Le Corbusier
A STUDY OF THE DECORATIVE ART MOVEMENT IN GERMANY

Edited by Mateo Kries
Translation by Alex T. Anderson

Vitra Design Museum

Editors: Mateo Kries, Alexander von Vegesack
Managing editor: Mateo Kries
Organisation: Claire Marie Rose, Anna Stüler
Translations: Alex T. Anderson, Jeremy Gaines
Copy editors: Jane Havell, Anna Stüler
Graphic design: Thorsten Romanus
Origination and printing: GZD, Ditzingen

Generously supported by the Department of Architecture at the
University of Washington, Seattle and by GZD, Ditzingen

The German National Library lists this title in the German National
Bibliography; detailed bibliographic information at http://dnb.ddb.de

ISBN 978-3-931936-29-7

www.design-museum.de

First edition 2008

CONTENTS

FOREWORD. Le Corbusier's influence on twentieth-century cultural life stems not only from his buildings and projects, but also from the numerous publications he brought out during the course of his life. The first of these, which appeared under his given name of Charles-Édouard Jeanneret, was *Étude sur le mouvement d'art décoratif en Allemagne*. The present book reprints this slender volume which first saw the light of day in 1912, along with scholarly commentaries.

Back in 1968, Stanislaus von Moos termed the *Étude* "one of the most masterful appreciations of the German applied arts movement", and it was also of immense biographical importance to Jeanneret himself. While in Germany, he matured from a traditionalist into a modern classicist and cosmopolitan, which he was essentially to remain for the rest of his life. The *Étude*, at first sight unassuming, contains many of the traits that were to become characteristic of the later Le Corbusier – ranging from his inclination to polemicise and polarise, via his self-stylisation as an artist-architect, to his lifelong search for his own identity. This oscillated somewhere between Mediterranean Classicism and his fascination for the industrial age, which he encountered in such emphatic form in Germany.

The present publication, designed to accompany the exhibition *Le Corbusier – The Art of Architecture*, also coincides with the centenary of the foundation of the Deutsche Werkbund. What better occasion to recall the highly interesting, exciting and at times controversial relationship between Le Corbusier and the German applied arts, indeed between German and French early Modernism *per se*?

The author would like to thank Alexander von Vegesack, Stanislaus von Moos, Philipp Ackermann, Alex T. Anderson, Michael Diers and Claire Rose, as well as Michel Richard, Isabelle Godineau and Arnaud Dercelles from the Fondation Le Corbusier, Paris, and especially Nadine Schemmann. Without their support this publication would not have been possible.

Basel and Berlin, March 2008
— *Mateo Kries*

Charles-Édouard Jeanneret, Villa Jeanneret-Perret, 1912. Jeanneret adopted the idea for the black window casements from Peter Behrens's crematorium in Hagen-Delstern, 1907. See p. 78

LE CORBUSIER IN GERMANY

— Mateo Kries

LE CORBUSIER IN GERMANY

"Your modern Germany is admirable, full of dedication, with energetic personal
courage on the part of citizens. France, by contrast, stones its prophets!
Do not hold it against me that I love France so!"
Charles-Édouard Jeanneret (Le Corbusier) to Karl Ernst Osthaus, 1912

In January 1910, the young architect Charles-Édouard
Jeanneret designed a strange building: a strictly symmetrical
group of cubes with flat roofs, with a central courtyard covered with a sloping roof. The whole design did not fit in at all
with the rather rural and folkloristic style of the few buildings
that Jeanneret had designed up to this date. Instead, astound-
ingly, it resembled a pavilion designed in 1905 by Peter
Behrens for an art exhibition in Oldenburg. On 29 February
1908, Jeanneret had written a rather negative comment on
German architecture to his teacher Charles L'Eplattenier:
"Frankly, what would you say if some day I worked in the
style of Kreis or Behrens...?"[1] Yet, a few months later, he
travelled to Berlin to work for several months in Behrens's
studio in Neubabelsberg. This episode is a good illustration of
the enormous increase in recognition and influence acquired
by the German applied arts around this time. The story of

Portrait of the Jeanneret family, Charles-Édouard sitting on the pedestal, **1889**   Jeanneret's *Étude sur le
mouvement d'art décoratif en Allemagne* gives a fascinating
insight into this development, and how it influenced his own
thoughts and designs in many ways.

Charles-Édouard Jeanneret's home town of La Chaux-
de-Fonds was one of Switzerland's industrial centres,
renowned for its clockmakers. In preparation for a career in
the clockmaking industry, he attended the local Arts and

Crafts College in 1902. In 1905, he switched to the newly founded *Cours Supérieur*, an advanced course in artistic training, where his most important teacher was Charles L'Eplattenier. L'Eplattenier influenced his students in the *style sapin* – a variant of Swiss Art Nouveau, in which regional and folkloristic elements were combined with a search for ornamentation derived from nature and with the reformist outlook of the British Arts and Crafts movement.[2] Jeanneret's early projects, such as the Villa Fallet of 1907, strictly championed this style, but he swiftly developed his own formal vocabulary which went beyond it. One reason for this was a series of trips abroad from 1907, during which he was able to study the historical role models and the latest artistic currents of the day. The first trip was to Italy; the second, in 1907–8, to Vienna.[3] In 1908–9, he spent longer periods in Paris, during which he also worked under Auguste Perret. In November 1909, he returned from Paris and spent the winter outside his home town in a Jurassic farmhouse. In La Chaux-de-Fonds he helped found the *Ateliers d'Art Réunis*, in which several graduates of the local arts and crafts college joined forces to produce and market their own designs, and to link teaching more closely to production. It was during this period that Jeanneret designed a building for the *Ateliers d'Art Réunis* with a striking resemblance to Behrens's pavilion.[4]

→ **Plate II**

Charles-Édouard Jeanneret, Villa Fallet, 1907

1 Stanislaus von Moos, *Le Corbusier – Elements of a Synthesis*, MIT Press, Cambridge, Mass. 1979, p. 36.
2 See Owen Jones, *The Grammar of Ornament*, Day and Sons, London, 1856; Eugène Viollet-le-Duc, *Dictionnaire raisonné de l'architecture française du XIe au XVIe siècle*, 10 vols, Bance, Paris, 1854–68; John Ruskin, *The Stones of Venice*, Smith, London, 1873.
3 See H. Allen Brooks, *Le Corbusier's Formative Years*, University of Chicago Press, Chicago/London, 1997, p. 253. In this book, Brooks provides the most exhaustive study to date of Jeanneret's travels as a youth and his stay in Germany. Even though Jeanneret later repeatedly mentioned that he worked for Josef Hoffmann in Vienna, this was not the case. He applied to work for Hoffmann and was accepted, but did not take up the job. See Brooks, pp. 117–50.
4 See on this Brooks, ibid., pp. 196–99.

Peter Behrens, exhibition hall for the North-West German Art Exhibition,
Oldenburg, 1905

La Chaux-de-Fonds, c. 1930. Photo: Walter Mittelholzer

Both the *Cours Supérieur* which Jeanneret attended and the *Ateliers d'Art Réunis* were part and parcel of the restructuring of the Art Academy in La Chaux-de-Fonds, which L'Eplattenier pushed through and in which Jeanneret was passionately involved. The idea was that the academy, which had trained fine craftsmen exclusively for clockmaking, would offer a broader range that responded to changes in the modern industrial world. A study of the German applied arts movement was commissioned to support this project, with the intention of highlighting the advantages of modernising the applied arts. L'Eplattenier managed to find a stipend to pay for the necessary research, and chose Jeanneret as the author – presumably because the latter's German was reasonable, he had stood out as an advocate of reform, and because in 1908 L'Eplattenier had already recommended that the young student round out his training by working with a German architect. The two men's hidden agenda for this stipend was a book project: they were planning a fundamental study on city planning under the title "La construction des villes", which they hoped would gain them great influence beyond their home town. In early April 1910, even before the stipend had been finally approved, Jeanneret departed for Munich to start his study trip.

→ **Plate III**

11

JEANNERET'S TRIPS TO GERMANY 1910–11

From La Chaux-de-Fonds, Jeanneret travelled via Karls-ruhe, Stuttgart and Ulm to Munich, where he applied for a position in Theodor Fischer's office, having admired his build-ings in Stuttgart and Ulm only a few days before.[5] Fischer taught urban planning at the Technical University in Munich and was a doyen of German reform architecture. Although he used modern materials and construction techniques, aestheti-cally he favoured a conservative position, with which Jean-neret at this point was in complete agreement. He failed to gain a position in Fischer's office owing to lack of space, but the contact thus established between them was to endure for years.[6] Jeanneret then found out that almost all the other well-known German architects – such as Peter Behrens, Bruno Paul, Hermann Muthesius and Heinrich Tessenow – were

Charles-Édouard Jeanneret, photograph of Nuremberg old town, 1910

based in Berlin. However, in-stead of paying them a visit, he spent the next few weeks ensconced in the Bavarian State Library primarily researching "La construction des villes", visited both Munich's museums and occasionally the opera. It was as if he had almost lost sight of the *Étude*. Not until the end of May, when official approval for the stipend was forthcoming and he had once again applied in vain to Fischer, did Jeanneret start serious research work on the *Étude*; he left for Berlin on the evening of 8 June 1910.

It was presumably Fischer who recommended that Jean-neret visit the Allgemeine Städtebau-Ausstellung (Exhibition

5 His address in Munich was Lotzbeckstrasse 3, 3rd Floor, and his housekeeper was Frau Vogt.
6 Theodor Fischer (1862–1938) had studied under Paul Wallot and was first presi-dent of the German Werkbund. Jeanneret received an invitation from him to a music afternoon in April 1910, which he described enthusiastically. Jeanneret remained in contact with Fischer, writing to congratulate him on his 75th birthday.

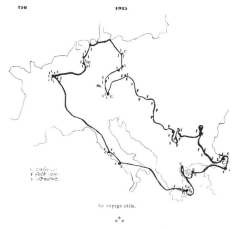

Le voyage utile.

Theodor Fischer, Protestant Garrison Church, Ulm, 1910

Le voyage utile – Jeanneret's travels from 1908 to 1911, published as an illustration
in *L'Art décoratif d'aujourd'hui*, Paris, 1925

of General Town Planning) in Berlin. But en route there, he heard from another person he had met fleetingly in Munich, Günther Freiherr von Pechmann, that the exhibition was only one of many events taking place in Berlin in the context of the third Werkbund Congress. This was a stroke of good fortune, affording Jeanneret the unique opportunity to gain an overall impression of the entire German applied arts scene in the space of only a few days. On the day of his arrival, he took part in a tour of the AEG buildings created by Peter Behrens, which included a product presentation, and in the next few days he viewed not only the Allgemeine Städtebau-Ausstellung but many other events which were to be decisive for the *Étude* and for his general development in the years to follow: the Ton-, Zement- und Kalkindustrie-Ausstellung, several lectures, various buildings by Bruno Paul and Hermann Muthesius, the Rheingold Restaurant designed by Bruno Schmitz, suburbs such as Nikolassee, Zehlendorf and Neu-Babelsberg, not to mention the Sanssouci Palace, the Applied

Charles-Édouard Jeanneret, orangery in the Sanssouci gardens, Potsdam, 1910. FLC

Arts Academy and its director Bruno Paul. He wrote enthusiastically to his parents about a performance of *A Midsummer Night's Dream* in the garden of the Muthesius House: "During my last few days here I have been very lucky. By chance I was able to take part in a congress of German artists, the Werkbund."[7] Jeanneret also sought employment with the architects he most preferred, applying on 16 June to Bruno Paul, on 18 June to Peter Behrens and that same day three times to Hermann Muthesius; but all his applications were in vain.

After attending all the Congress events a second time, Jeanneret set off back to Munich on 21 June.[8] His route was via Wittenberg, Halle, Naumburg and Weimar (where, to his

7 Postcard to his parents, 13 June 1910, Bibliothèque de la Ville de La Chaux-de-Fonds (BV).

14

regret, he missed meeting the founder and director of the art academy there, Henry van de Velde). He travelled on via Jena, Coburg, Lichtenfels, Bamberg and Würzburg, arriving in Munich on the evening of 25 June. In a letter to his parents of 29 June, he described himself as a starving student, exhausted by his travels, but nevertheless said that the last three months had been the "most fulfilling in my life".[9] In the same letter he reported that on 28 June he had made the acquaintance of a student called Auguste Klipstein, with whom he was now practising his German conversational skills. After the art critic and author William Ritter, whom he had met in Munich at the end of May, Klipstein was Jeanneret's second important acquaintance in the city. The following year they travelled together through the Balkans to Istanbul, and remained close friends for years.[10]

Charles-Édouard Jeanneret, self-portrait in a letter to William Ritter, 29 June 1910

Jeanneret immersed himself in life in Munich with renewed zest, visiting the Summer Trade Fair (where he saw an exhibition on Islamic art) and viewing buildings such as the Villa Leibl and the Villa Stuck. At the end of July he hiked via Mittenwald into the Alps and thence home to La Chaux-de-Fonds, where he spent the summer.

8 Jeanneret subsequently added an exact list of activities on all days in his diary, emphasising the importance he attached to his time in Berlin. An excerpt: "Saturday Town Planning Exhibition. 4 1/2 hours Railway Station. Then hotel, evening meal and wine restaurant Rheingold. Sunday Linden. Limestone-Cement-Clay Exhibition, lecture – then hotel, lecture – then hotel and Nikolassee (Midsummer Night's Dream)/Monday w. Schneider in Greater Berlin Exh. 2 hours meal, print-ready drawing of sketch of Muthesius. 4 1/2 Bismarckstrasse/Café Secession." Quoted from Giuliano Gresleri, ed., *Le Corbusier, Les voyages d'Allemagne – Carnets*, Electa, Milan/Fondation Le Corbusier, Paris, 1994, Carnet I.
9 Letter to his parents, 29 June 1910, Nationalbibliothek Bern.
10 Auguste Klipstein (1885–1951) studied art history in Munich. Jeanneret visited him the following year in his home town of Laubach, outside Frankfurt, where he planned a house for Klipstein's brother in 1914. For details on the trip to the east Jeanneret and Klipstein made, see Giuliano Gresleri, *Le Corbusier, Viaggio in Oriente*, Marsilio, Venice, 1984.

The second part of Jeanneret's stay in Germany in 1910 commenced on 17 September, when he again left La Chaux-de-Fonds for Munich. He was now hoping to get a job under Peter Behrens in Berlin, having sent a written application. After a couple of weeks in Munich with no reply, he lost patience and set out for Berlin on 17 October, to find that Behrens had fallen ill and he would have to wait even longer for a response. He used the time between 21 and 25 October to visit Dresden, where his brother had accepted a post under the dance teacher Émile Jaques-Dalcroze. On returning to Berlin, Jeanneret at long last received the green light from Behrens. He started on 1 November as a technical draftsman in the studio in Babelsberg: the first – and last – full-time job of his entire life. He spent Christmas 1910 with Albert in Dresden, and by spring 1911 was already planning for life after Behrens. He and Auguste Klipstein prepared for their trip to Istanbul, intending to start from Dresden in May.[11] Before that, he wished to travel the length and breadth of Germany for a second time, to collect the last batch of infor-

Dresden station concourse, c. 1910. Jeanneret travelled to Dresden by train to visit his brother in Hellerau garden city in 1910–11

mation for the *Étude*. Ending his employment in Behrens's studio on 1 April 1911, he went first to Dresden and then, on 7 April, to Munich. He left on 19 April for Stuttgart, Karlsruhe, Heidelberg, Darmstadt and Frankfurt, and arrived in Laubach on 24 April to visit Klipstein at his parents' house to discuss preparations for their trip. He left Laubach on 5 May, this time bound for Cologne by steamer, and from there travelled on to Düsseldorf, Hagen, Bremen, Hamburg, Lübeck and Lüneburg. The round trip ended in Berlin on Saturday, 13 May. On 20 May, Jeanneret went to Dresden where he met up with Klipstein. Together, they left for Prague

11 Letters to Auguste Klipstein, 12 February and 10 March 1911, Fondation Le Corbusier (FLC).

on 24 May, the first stop on their long-awaited eastern tour. He returned, via Greece and Italy, on 1 November, then headed home to La Chaux-de-Fonds. All in all, he had been away for 18 months, discounting his spell at home in the summer of 1910.

Charles-Édouard Jeanneret, photographic self-portrait in his room in Neubabelsberg, April 1911. Drawings from trips he made to Italy and France in 1907–9 are hanging on the walls

GENESIS OF THE ÉTUDE

The pattern of Jeanneret's stay in Germany shows that the effort he put into working on the *Étude* was anything but hasty. But the zealous student in search of knowledge was interested in many other projects, including the text of "La construction des villes", finding employment under Behrens, his trip to Istanbul, magazine articles and a search for distribution for *Ateliers d'Art* products. Moreover, research for the *Étude* did not follow a constant scheme. Lengthy stays in Munich and Berlin were followed by a few intense trips during which Jeanneret enthusiastically absorbed new knowledge and completely exhausted himself; he then returned to a withdrawn life, working up his drawings and notes, visiting museums and the opera, and corresponding at great length. It is therefore hardly surprising that on several occasions he put back the date for completion of his text. This was probably originally planned for the end of 1910, but after the summer he was talking of April 1911 as the deadline. In a lengthy letter to L'Eplattenier of 16 January 1911 he drew up large parts of the introductory chapter,[12] but in a subsequent missive of

"Cupido 80" camera, which Jeanneret bought in May 1911

4–7 May he informed his teacher that he had decided to travel to Istanbul, which made completion of the *Étude* impossible at that time. He excused himself cursorily by saying that the stipend had not been limited to a specific period.[13]

Only after his return to La Chaux-de-Fonds in November 1911 did Jeanneret finally sit down to write the text. Since by this time he was able to resort to any amount of notes and diary entries, it is probable that the work mainly involved sorting and formulating passages of text. The body of the text

12 Letter to L'Eplattenier, 16 January 1911, FLC.
13 Letter to L'Eplattenier, 4–7 May 1911, FLC.

18

was complete by early 1912 and was presented to the Art Academy's Commission on 22 February. It was greeted so positively that publication was decided on, although this had not been planned originally. The book was published by Haefeli in La Chaux-de-Fonds, in an initial edition of 500 copies. Most of these were sent to dignitaries, with very few finding their way into bookshops. Two years later, the core of the *Étude* (excluding the introduction, which was more personal in tone) was reprinted in the journal *L'Œuvre*, the mouthpiece of the French-speaking section of the Swiss Werkbund which, after returning from Germany, Jeanneret himself played a part in setting up.[14]

→ **Plate XVI**

POWER POLITICS AND APPLIED ARTS – EN ROUTE TO THE WERKBUND

If the *Étude* had been written just ten years earlier it would no doubt have focused more on England or Austria, since around 1900 these countries were considered far more progressive than Germany.[15] But after the turn of the century Germany took a leading role in the international applied arts scene. Jeanneret described how this came about in his "General Considerations" at the beginning of the *Étude*. The fact that he juxtaposed Germany and France not only reflected his personal perspective as a Francophile Swiss but also the general political situation. The two countries' struggle for

---

14 Charles-Édouard Jeanneret, "Le renouveau dans l'architecture", in *L'Œuvre*, vol. 1, no. 2, 1914, pp. 33–37.
15 In England, following the spread of the ideas of William Morris and John Ruskin, it was above all Charles Rennie Mackintosh and Charles F. Voysey who established the country's international reputation as a pioneer of modern design. In Austria, around 1900 and partly stimulated by developments in England, the school of so-called Vienna architects emerged; its protagonists included Josef Hoffmann, Otto Wagner and Joseph Maria Olbrich.

domination of the European continent during the entire nineteenth century had ensured that their opposition was embedded as a kind of basic conflict in the European collective consciousness. After their defeats in the Napoleonic Wars at the beginning of the nineteenth century, the Germans made arduous efforts to unite the Reich between 1848 and 1866 and emerged the victors in the 1870–71 war against France. Germany then annexed Alsace-Lorraine, not far from Jeanneret's canton. And the Reich was able to present impressive figures in other areas, too: between 1871 and 1913, the German population grew from 41 to 67 million people; in Berlin alone the population almost doubled from 1.88 million in 1900 to 3.73 million in 1910. The real income earned by a worker rose from 466 Reichsmarks in 1871 to 834 in 1913. In 1910, Germany had a good 61,000 km of rail track, whereas France had just over 40,000 km. In short, after 1871 Germany emerged as a European super-power and, at the same time, as a threat to the carefully calibrated, centuries-old balance of power between England, France and Russia.

→ Plate I

Many pointed comments in the *Étude* show that Jeanneret rejected Prussian power politics, and this message is conveyed even more sharply in his diary entries and letters. He noted on one of his trips around Germany, after seeing the fraternity monument designed by Wilhelm Kreis in Eisenach: "I have never seen anything as malformed and awfully anti-aesthetic as these towers in the countryside on the hills. Be it Bismarck Column or viewing platform, however simple they may be, they are not some crowning achievement."[16] Nevertheless, Jeanneret recognised in the *Étude* that the Prussian inclination to opt for naive symbols of power went hand-in-hand with a highly successful politics of modernisation which

---

16 Gresleri, ed., *Le Corbusier, Les voyages d'Allemagne – Carnets*, op. cit., Carnet IV, p. 1.

20

Thyssen-Krupp at the Paris World's Fair, 1867

Caricature "Parade auf dem Tempelhofer Damm" in *Simplicissimus*, 1912–3

formed the central precondition for the upturn in German arts and crafts. Germany's backwardness in the applied arts had become shockingly apparent at the London Great Exhibition of 1851. Gottfried Semper was the first to call for a drastic improvement in "education in taste" and in training in the arts and crafts.[17] The first museums of applied arts were established, doubling up as teaching colleges and attracting public interest in the importance of the applied arts. The liberalisation of the Reich after Bismarck's resignation in 1890 created a social environment that boosted the applied arts further. Journals such as *Die Hilfe*, *Simplicissimus* and *Die Jugend* became important voices of the artistic avant-garde which, in the domain of the applied arts, initially flocked to the banner of Art Nouveau. The most impressive demonstration of this movement was the Mathildenhöhe artists' colony in Darmstadt. On the international scene, Germany's presence at the world expositions in 1900 in Paris and in 1904 in St Louis helped to improve the international reputation of German designers.

Poster for the third German Applied Arts Exhibition, Dresden, 1906

In the years after 1900 it became more noticeable that German applied arts were starting to develop beyond Art Nouveau. At the Applied Arts Exhibition organised by Fritz Schumacher in 1906 in Dresden, sober furniture typologies and houses for workers clearly attested to the fact that a new industrial aesthetics was emerging which had nothing in common with the ornamental French movement. In a lecture at the exhibition, the politician Friedrich Naumann commented on this new trend:

> Reproduction is a fundamental idea of industrial art. Germany now has a number of high-ranking commercial artists who have a national status overall, something we have not previously had. This is not coincidence. As long as we focused on arts and crafts in the old sense, there could be ingenious crafts-

---

17 Gottfried Semper, *Kleine Schriften*, Spemann, Berlin, 1884.

men, whose efforts will survive for centuries, but artists who define an entire epoch and whose hand can be sensed directly or indirectly in tens of thousands of flats are only just on the ascent. ... Machine furniture does not evolve overnight out of old artistic craftsmanship, but only gradually does everything change in the direction of simple mechanical reproduceability.[18]

Almost at the same time, Naumann discussed with Hermann Muthesius, Fritz Schumacher and Karl Schmidt the idea of founding a new alliance of designers with a modern focus, and proposed that Wolf Dohrn be brought on board to organise it – a young man from a prosperous family who had prime contacts in the worlds of finance and industry.[19] The final foundation of the Werkbund and thus of a quasi-official organ for the applied arts movement was set in motion when Hermann Muthesius held a lecture at Berlin's Handelshochschule, the College of Commerce, in 1907, sharply criticising traditional arts and crafts:

The use of external trimmings as in the old styles of art is now no longer on the agenda, people are endeavouring to speak a new, unique, independent artistic language. ... Thus the main thrust of modern applied arts has arisen, namely first to decide very clearly what the purpose of each object is and then to develop the form logically from that purpose. Following a design in line with the purpose comes a design in line with the material's properties, and a consideration for the material spelled a consideration of a construction commensurate with the material. ... By simple logic a principle has in this way been restored to currency that had almost got lost in the cogs of nineteenth-century industrial

18 Friedrich Naumann, "Kunst und Industrie", lecture at the 3rd German Applied Arts Exhibition in Dresden, published in Kurt Junghanns, *Der Deutsche Werkbund: sein erstes Jahrzehnt*, Henschelverlag, Berlin, 1982, pp. 137–39.
19 Wolf Dohrn (1878–1914) was born in Naples and studied in Berlin and Leipzig before moving to Munich. There, he studied under Lujo von Brentano and made friends with Theodor Heuss, later to be Germany's President, who was a supporter of the Werkbund from an early date. Friedrich Naumann (1860–1919) met Dohrn during his work for the journal *Die Hilfe* in Munich, which Naumann had founded. His father was the scientist Anton Dohrn (1840–1909), who had a building designed by Adolf Hildebrand in Naples for the Zoological Station he had founded; Hans von Marées painted several frescoes in his private residence there.

Peter Behrens, "Hamburger Halle" at the exhibition of modern decorative arts
for the World Exposition, Turin, 1902. The photograph was published by Le Corbusier
in *L'Art décoratif d'aujourd'hui* 1925

Henry van de Velde, museum hall at the third German Applied Arts Exhibition,
Dresden, 1906. The wall painting is by Ludwig von Hofman

production. … Social pretensions arose in the battle of the social classes for supremacy. The bourgeoisie that had already gained significance felt a need for ostentation, which it was only able to satisfy with external, less expensive means.[20]

Muthesius's polemical attack caused a scandal. The forces of tradition sought to have him fired from his position in the Ministry of Trade, while the Dresdner Werkstätten and several other companies withdrew from the Berlin association that lobbied on behalf of the commercial arts. Plans for a new association therefore had to be moved forward swiftly. Wolf Dohrn was commissioned to make preparations for the foundation of the Werkbund, which officially took place in Munich on 5–6 October 1907. He compiled an exhaustive memorandum and a draft set of statutes for the first Members' Meeting, which took place on 12 July 1908, also in Munich. While Theodor Fischer as the first president essentially discharged representational duties on behalf of the Werkbund, Dohrn as the secretary general was the organisational

Wolf Dohrn, founding charter of the Deutscher Werkbund, 1908

driving force. Dohrn had also been of indispensable assistance to Karl Schmidt in Dresden in advancing the plans for the Hellerau Garden City project, and the members decided to locate the Werkbund's office in Dresden.

Charles-Édouard Jeanneret's first personal contact with the Werkbund developed in 1910 in Munich, through Theodor Fischer. He probably met the young Wolf Dohrn at the Werkbund Congress in Berlin at a reception at Hermann Muthesius's house. Dohrn was Jeanneret's key source of information on the Werkbund, and the two men no doubt met on several occasions during Jeanneret's later visits to Hellerau. It was probably Dohrn who gave Jeanneret a copy of the statutes and the other programmatic Werkbund texts, from which he then proceeded to quote, in part verbatim, in the

---

20 Hermann Muthesius, "Die Bedeutung des Kunstgewerbes", lecture in the Berlin College of Commerce, quoted from Junghanns, *Die Bedeutung des Kunstgewerbes*, op. cit., pp. 139–40.

Étude.[21] Detailed information on membership figures and Werkbund committees also suggests that Dohrn provided extensive data.

Thanks to a rapid increase in membership in the early years of 1908–10, the Werkbund had changed from a secessionist movement into something that was almost the official organ of the German applied arts world. Given such swift growth, there was inevitably tension, not to mention battles over direction. Wolf Dohrn resigned as secretary general at the Berlin Congress of 1910, raising the question that Jeanneret might have heard critical remarks from him on the Werkbund's future prospects. This hypothesis is suggested by Jeanneret's own critique at the end of the *Étude* of the politicisation and lack of depth of the Werkbund. Even if this was a coincidence, Jeanneret at any rate had discerned a basic conflict in the Werkbund which was to become even fiercer in the years to come. Dohrn's successor Alphons Paquet was replaced as secretary general in 1912 by Ernst Jäckh, who

Peter Behrens, poster for the Werkbund exhibition, Cologne, 1914

relocated the Werkbund's office to Berlin and forged even closer links with politics. Although the Werkbund continued to grow – by 1915 it had 1,972 members – the criticism endured that it was being appropriated and was turning its back on the secessionist ideals that had led to its foundation.

21 Thus the verbatim quotations in the first sentence of the chapter on the Werkbund in the *Étude* are based on Article 2 of the Founding Articles of the German Werkbund of 12 July 1908. The articles and other programmatic writings from the founding years are to be found in Junghanns, *Der Deutsche Werkbund*, op. cit., pp. 137 ff.

22 Karl Ernst Osthaus (1874–1921) came from a prosperous banking family and was a major patron of Early Modernism in Germany. Having sympathised with nationalist, conservative ideas at the end of the nineteenth century, a series of articles by Julius Meier-Graefe on Henry van de Velde in the magazine *Dekorative Kunst* in 1900 made him an ardent supporter of Modernist views. Osthaus's activities ranged from the applied arts to the visual arts to theatre. See Herta Hesse-Frielinghaus, ed., et. al., *Karl Ernst Osthaus: Leben und Werk*, Recklinghausen, Bongers, 1971.

MUSEUM REFORM AND TRAVELLING EXHIBITIONS

Jeanneret also had a key contact in Germany when it came to studying the second initiative in the field of "Organisation and Propaganda", the Museum für Kunst und Gewerbe in Hagen, namely Karl Ernst Osthaus.[22] Osthaus was a member of the Werkbund's Board and, as a patron and organiser, a central figure in Germany's cultural life. Jeanneret heard him lecture at the Werkbund Congress in Berlin on "Material and Style". Back in Berlin in October 1910, waiting to start work for Behrens,

Sign for the Deutsches Museum für Kunst in Handel und Gewerbe, 1909

Jeanneret visited the first show held at the Museum für Kunst in Handel und Gewerbe. Entitled "Die Kunst in Dienste des Händlers", it was shown at the Hohenzollern furniture store. Jeanneret recorded his reactions in his notebook, and the second section of this passage was then incorporated into the *Étude*:

It is an exhibition with everything relating to advertising, posters, letterheads, etc. There is something of everything, e.g., Kunstgewerbeschule Vienna makes sweet tins with a colour lithograph on the lid showing art cities and what is most typical for them. Such as the Zwinger in Dresden or the Baumwall in Hamburg. ... The Wiener Werkstätten have designed the packaging for the Cida brand of chocolate, there are a good 12 different motifs. On show are also advertisements from newspapers, advertisements that set out to fulfil artistic standards. ... The exhibition is made up of several small rooms. The original drawings and the printed matter are glued on anthracite grey/green paper, all cut to the same size.[23]

Another note during the Berlin Congress shows that the name Osthaus did not yet mean anything to Jeanneret: "There is a museum, the Deutsches Museum für Kunst in Handel und Gewerbe Hagen i. W., founded by the man who also spoke at

23 See *Le Corbusier, Les voyages d'Allemagne – Carnets*, op. cit., Carnet III, pp. 69–71.

the Allgemeine Bau-, Zement- und Kalkindustrieausstellung. I should gather information for my report there, find out how artists were treated, etc."[24] A few months later Jeanneret realised this objective when he visited Osthaus in Hagen on 9 May 1911. There he saw a second exhibition organised by the museum, this time on hairstyles and the art of hairdressing worldwide, something he again described in the *Étude*. At the same time, Jeanneret gained an idea of Osthaus's many other activities with which he had so shaped the "Hagen stimulus". In 1898, he had founded the Museum Folkwang for which he had a building designed in the historicist style by Berlin architect and Government councillor Carl Gérard. Henry van de Velde was commissioned to design the interior – a volte-face in terms of design. In 1907–8, van de Velde designed Osthaus's private villa, the Hohenhof; he also introduced him to the art dealers Ambroise Vollard and Paul Cassirer. He wrote of Osthaus: "in less than a year he had acquired works by Monet, Renoir, Seurat, Signac, Cross, van Gogh and Gauguin as well as sculptures by Minne, Rodin and Constantin Meunier."[25] In 1903–5, Peter Behrens designed a lecture hall for the Museum Folkwang and in 1907 a crematorium in Hagen's Delstern district. Another project Osthaus undertook was a garden city in Hagen's suburb of Eppenhausen which, in the space of only a few years, featured the Cuno and Schröder residences, both designed by Behrens, as well as buildings by Lauweriks and a workers' estate by Richard Riemerschmid.

24 Ibid., p. 68.
25 See Hans Curjel, *Henry van de Velde: Geschichte meines Lebens* (1962), repr. Piper, Munich, 1986, pp. 217–18.

The "Hagen Hall" at the German Applied Arts Exhibition, Dresden, 1906

The "German Applied Arts" exhibition by the Deutsche Museum für Kunst in
Handel und Gewerbe, held at the National Arts Club, New York, 1913

Peter Behrens, crematorium in Hagen-Delstern, 1907

Osthaus proved with the Museum Folkwang that he was one of the key German museum reformers. He proceeded to transpose these ideas to applied arts in the form of the Museum für Kunst in Handel und Gewerbe. Unlike nineteenth-century arts and crafts museums with their collections of specimens, Osthaus, as Jeanneret emphasised twice in the *Étude*, called for a museum which "traces a better picture of our own epoch" and championed the principle of touring exhibitions:

> Museums once delicately turned their backs on vibrant life, but have now grasped the tasks of the day and made exhibitions a permanent feature in all major cities. ... The task falls to exhibitions of familiarising the public with the movement's intentions. They have inserted themselves as the factor regulating taste between the dealers and the buyers. ... There are museums that have almost exhausted their budgets with exhibitions. It would be a waste to continue this effort in terms of time, money and energy. The field of exhibitions must be organised. With the same work that an exhibition requires, twenty could be prepared, if only a central agency was in charge of the organisational work.[26]

The objects chosen for the Deutsches Museum were collected in Hagen's Museum Folkwang, archived and then assembled to form exhibitions. From 1909–10 alone, about 10,000 items of printed matter were collected. Thanks to its alliance with the Werkbund, the new museum could immediately rely on a functioning network and countless collaborators who hosted touring exhibitions the length and breadth of Germany. In 1910–14, exhibitions by the Museum Folkwang went on show at a total of 200 venues, including four displays during the Cologne Werkbund Exhibition in 1914. The most important international initiative was a tour of the United States by the "German Applied Arts" exhibition, which was showcased at many different museums in 1912–13.[27]

26 See Karl Ernst Osthaus, "Das Deutsche Museum für Kunst in Handel und Gewerbe", *Die Welt des Kaufmanns*, vol. 5, 10 October 1909, p. 468.

When visiting Hagen, Jeanneret not only acquired the exhaustive information to which his report on the Deutsches Museum in the *Étude* bears witness. He and Osthaus doubtless shared many pursuits, including a passion for French painting, for Paris and for the east which, for example, Osthaus had referenced in his lecture at the Werkbund Congress in 1910 and which Jeanneret had jotted down with interest.[28] Moreover, as early as 1913 Osthaus started presenting pictures by van Gogh, Matisse and Gaugin at the Museum Folkwang, synoptically with non-European art – a principle that is strongly reminiscent of Le Corbusier's later preference for combining art and objects of various origins in line with his principle of *synthèse des arts*. Given all these links, it is no surprise that on 28 July 1911 Jeanneret wrote to Osthaus from Istanbul: "how strongly I was touched by the reception at your house".[29] A letter to Osthaus of 27 March 1912 attests to there being an open exchange on the Franco-German relationship and is emblematic of Jeanneret's ambivalent stance to Germany *per se*:

→ Plate VI

> Yes, in my report I mentioned your admirable work in Germany. Your modern Germany is admirable, full of dedication, with energetic personal courage on the part of citizens. France, by contrast, stones its prophets! Do not hold it against me that I love France so! France is the country of smiles and of the good life. It is the radiant and balanced people. … I shall take the liberty of sending you my report as soon as it has come out.[30]

27 The exhibition toured to The Newark Museum Association, Newark, New Jersey; The City Art Museum, St Louis, Missouri; The Art Institute of Chicago, Chicago, Illinois; The John Herron Art Institute, Indianapolis, Indiana; The Cincinnati Museum Association, Cincinnati, Ohio, and The Carnegie Institute, Pittsburgh, Pennsylvania.
28 See *Le Corbusier, Les voyages d'Allemagne – Carnets*, op. cit., Carnet I, pp. 19–21.
29 Letter to Karl Ernst Osthaus, 28 July 1911, quoted from Jean Jenger, op. cit., p. 86.
30 Letter to Karl Ernst Osthaus, 27 March 1912, ibid., p. 95.

APPLIED ARTS AS A COMPETITIVE EDGE

While the Deutscher Werkbund and Deutsches Museum für Kunst und Gewerbe were expressly federal initiatives, in the following sections of the *Étude* Jeanneret took a series of initiatives with a partly proud local thrust as the object of investigation. The fact that he chose Munich as a case study probably reflects his own preference for the Baroque city with its Mediterranean touch. In comparison with the strict Prussianness of Berlin, Munich was considered a centre of German Bohemians and a city infused with *joie de vivre*. At the turn of the twentieth century, Munich was also home to German Art Nouveau. Peter Behrens, Bruno Paul and Richard Riemerschmid had lived there; the key journals of German Art Nouveau, *Simplicissimus* and *Die Hilfe*, were published there, and the Deutscher Werkbund was founded there in 1908, the year that Jeanneret stopped off en route for Vienna. With the end of Art Nouveau and the emergence of a new, more matter-of-fact approach to design, Munich found itself facing serious rivalry in the form of other German cities. It

Charles-Édouard Jeanneret, photograph of the Theatine Church, Munich, April 1910

was thus challenged to incorporate its many artists into the new alliance of industry and art for, as Jeanneret wrote: "Munich has thousands of artists", but "life has been made difficult, in recent years, for the poet who varnishes canvases but forgets to sell them…"[31]

The applied arts offered a promising perspective, demonstrated in 1908 by the Bavarian Applied Arts section's presentation at the Paris Salon d'Automne, which Jeanneret recorded in his diary as "having had the pleasure to follow in the Parisian papers".[32] Shortly afterwards, an Agency for

31 Charles-Édouard Jeanneret, *Étude sur le mouvement d'art décoratif en Allemagne*, Haefeli, La Chaux-de-Fonds, 1912. Quoted on p. 163.
32 *Le Corbusier, Les voyages d'Allemagne – Carnets*, op. cit., Carnet III, pp. 10–11.

Charles-Édouard Jeanneret, sketch of the St Kajetan Theatine Church, Munich, 1911.
Pencil on paper, FLC

Applied Arts was founded in Munich to modernise the applied arts in the state and improve how the arts presented themselves, tasks that required management by someone with a strong network and the necessary influence. The brief was tailor-made for its founder, Günter von Pechmann, as it was for Dohrn in Hellerau and Osthaus in Hagen. Von Pechmann also came from a prosperous family and embodied the blend of patron, entrepreneur and functionary characteristic of the applied arts movement. Alongside his activities for the agency he was also a board member of both the Werkbund and the Deutsche Werkstätten.[33] Jeanneret presumably first met von Pechmann shortly before 28 April 1910, possibly through Theodor Fischer, his first point of contact in Munich. As we can glean from Jeanneret's correspondence, at that first meeting not only did he discuss information for the *Étude*, but also the issue of whether the agency would include in its range some of the products manufactured by *Ateliers d'Art*.[34] He wrote to his friend Leon Perrin in La Chaux-de-Fonds on 28 April requesting him to send some specimen products urgently, but nothing came of it.

In autumn 1910, Jeanneret had the opportunity to study another initiative with which the city wished to use the applied arts to gain a competitive edge – the "Exhibition Munich". A trade fair ground had been created on the Theresienwiese in 1908 on the occasion of the 750th anniversary of the Free State of Bavaria; it consisted of numerous pavilions which were henceforth used each year for new events. The fourth German Applied Arts exhibition, entitled "Rejuvenating Furniture", was held there during the first fair, as was the first meeting of the Werkbund. In summer 1910, the next major exhibition to follow was "Islamic Art",

33 Günther Freiherr von Pechmann was later also Director of the Königlich Preussische Porzellan-Manufaktur in Berlin.
34 Letter to Leon Perrin, 28 April 1910, FLC.

which Jeanneret visited in mid-September shortly after returning to Munich from his summer vacation in La Chaux-de-Fonds. He visited the "Exhibition Munich" again on 8 October to view the puppet theatre set up that year by Paul Ludwig Troost (1878–1934), which greatly impressed him with its restrained classicism. Presumably this was what Jeanneret referred to in the *Étude* when commenting favourably on the overall trade fair ground and the buildings there.[35] When he went to Munich again in April 1911, preparations were already under

way for the next

Matthias Feller, entrance of the Ballin furniture store, Munich, 1909. Jeanneret visited it during his travels and mentioned it as closely associated with the Werkbund

event in 1912. An "Organisational Directorate for the Bavarian Trades Show" had been formed, in which Pechmann's "Agency for the Applied Arts", the Munich Kunstgewerbeverein, the "Exhibition Park" Association and the "Society for the Preservation of Art" had joined forces. Jeanneret, a skilled networker, had established closer personal links with Pechmann, and had gleaned this information while dining with him. Jeanneret's diary notes offer an insight into the aims of the event and also show that, behind the scenes, not everyone was working together:

> Extra magazine for the new show to prepare the public; edited by Pechmann. … Association for Popular Art and Local Knowledge for the Preservation of Local Art (retrograde, reactionary in tendency as rural art draws everything from the city and is dying out. So Pechmann and others' theory.) … The goal: to establish a rival to the Leipzig Trade Fair, which is overcrowded. To organise a fair, but to select from everything that is art. Preparations for a conference, Pechmann shows that Munich is predestined to assume this role (art, less critical industry, influx from abroad). An effort will be made to attract all wholesalers from the United States and elsewhere.[36]

35 Quoted on p. 167 f.
36 *Le Corbusier, Les voyages d'Allemagne – Carnets*, op. cit., Carnet IV, pp. 14–6.

Bruno Paul, poster for an applied arts exhibition at the Altes National Museum in Munich (now Alte Nationalgalerie), 1901

As these notes show, Munich wished with its trade fair and applied arts world to attract the flow of "events tourists" which had already commenced with the world expositions in preceding decades. In the next passage, Jeanneret used the occasion to formulate some general thoughts on federalism and rivalry among German cities. It was a fact that within the still young federal system cities and regions were competing fiercely for applied arts institutions, events and contracts. On the one hand, municipal representatives such as von Pechmann condemned the "retrograde, reactionary tendencies" of rural art; on the other, it was often the representatives of the applied arts who were members of guilds in the cities who championed traditional art. They were facing competition from the new industrialised furniture makers, as the journal *Innendekoration* recorded from a Berlin perspective in 1909:

Customary warehouse goods are already being knocked together in the cheap provinces. Yet even large orders are increasingly being placed outside, and reputed companies such as Pössenbacher, Ballin and Vereinigten Werkstätten in Munich, Deutsche Werkstätten Dresden, Schultze-Naumburg's Saalecker Werkstätten, Schneider & Hanau in Frankfurt, Harrod's Stores (invited by the Kaiser, no less) set up local branches advertising their wares. The province was more active than the capital, certainly. The impressive shows in Dresden, Munich, Darmstadt and smaller venues have always, partly successful or not, caused a great stir, and were a great promotion for the cities and the applied arts there. ... A show with works by Paul, Schmitz, Behrens, Muthesius, Geßner, Möhring, Mohrbutter, Grenander, Schaudt, Kaufmann, Henker, Wünsche, Caroli, Staumer, Landsberg, Seeck, Krüger and many other assiduous talents – such a show of the best would have been able to compete in terms of importance with the Darmstadt, Munich and Dresden exhibitions and would no doubt have been to the benefit of Berlin's reputation as a citadel of art. Such a show must and will take place sooner or later if Berlin is not to lag behind forever.[37]

37 See *Innendekoration*, vol. XX, September 1909, n.p.

36

Jeanneret himself appreciated some of the individual buildings created by Bruno Paul and Albert Gessner in Berlin, as well as the "garden cities" of Zehlendorf and Frohnau, but overall Munich, with its nineteenth-century classicism, remained his favourite German city. He revered the buildings designed by Theodor Fischer, but was also full of praise for Emmanuel von Seidl's Villa Brakl, which he visited in autumn 1910. The house had "much of the traditional, and is thus spacious and powerful, calm, while those in Berlin are dry and workmanlike. ... Although there is none of the English (pre-Raphaelite) comfort of a Muthesius, and it is less spectacular than a Bruno Paul, it has great scope."[38]

→ Plates IV + V

THREE INFLUENTIAL EXHIBITIONS

The Werkbund Congress in 1910 was the occasion for an "impressive show", as the writer in *Innendekoration* had called for in Berlin in 1909. With the many associated events, Berlin emphasised its status as the centre for German applied arts. The General Town Planning Exhibition outlined this in the field of urbanism: Berlin was seeking both to represent its role as the Reich's capital city in the domain of town planning and also to solve the pressing problems of a sturdy influx of new inhabitants. In 1909 two Berlin architectural associations had launched a "Competition for the Master Plan for Building Greater Berlin". The objective was to forge a plan for the development of the sprawling city and to reorganise the outer suburbs. Solutions were needed for socially run-down residential districts, such as providing public green spaces and introducing modern transportation technology; the city was to be given an imperial look. Entries were to assume a total of

38 *Le Corbusier, Les voyages d'Allemagne – Carnets*, op. cit., Carnet III, pp. 26, 33.

five million inhabitants. The 27 submissions were showcased in the "Greater Berlin" exhibition, which formed the first section of the General Town Planning Exhibition in 1910. The second section presented exemplary projects from other cities which placed the Berlin ideas in an international context. The entire exhibition was curated by Werner Hegemann, who also edited the accompanying guide.[39]

Jeanneret attended the international part of the show on his first day after arriving in Berlin, 11 June 1910; he looked at the section with the competition entries on "Greater Berlin" two days later. He visited both again a few days afterwards. His response to the show was a mixture of being impressed and feeling ambivalent. In Möhring's garden city concept, which he sketched in his notebook, he discerned street lines that "are quite unlike the official geometric versions".[40] By contrast, he commented on Bruno Schmitz's project for a round high-rise between Potsdamer Platz and Leipziger Platz: "Bruno Schmitz, who has a weakness for things colossal, envisages a gigantic skyscraper that could become a major landmark (as it is beautiful)."[41] On the international examples, he commented in his diary: "The French have contributed nothing. The Americans Chicago and other cities (it's awful). The Danes little. The Dutch a few good things."[42] His judgments in the *Étude* were equally ambiguous. On the one hand, he still found the German contributions best on an international comparison, but his admiration

39 *Führer durch die Allgemeine Städtebau-Ausstellung in Berlin 1910*, Wasmuth, Berlin, 1910, and Werner Hegemann, *Der Städtebau nach den Ergebnissen der allgemeinen Städtebau-Ausstellung in Berlin*, inc. appendix, *Die internationale Städtebau-Ausstellung in Düsseldorf*, Wasmuth, Berlin, 1911. Jeanneret acquired two copies of the guidebook in order to send one to William Ritter in Munich. On the 1910 General Town Planning Exhibition, see Josef Paul Kleihues, ed., et. al., *Bauen in Berlin 1900–2000*, Nicolai, Berlin, 2000, p. 53.
40 *Le Corbusier, Les voyages d'Allemagne – Carnets*, op. cit., Carnet I, pp. 56–79.
41 Ibid., p. 65.
42 Ibid., p. 75.

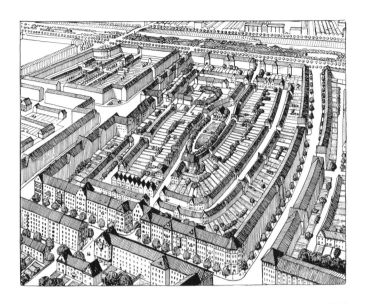

Bruno Möhring, brochure for a garden city for the "Greater Berlin" competition, 1910

Charles-Édouard Jeanneret, photograph of a courtyard house in
Berlin's Zehlendorf district, June 1910

39

Bruno Schmitz, study for a tower building on Leipziger Platz, Berlin, 1909

was coloured by scepticism towards the thirst for things colossal, a characteristic feature of German architecture: "it was huge, gigantic, impressive and perhaps even very beautiful. There one observed men now capable of confronting any problem. Berlin wants to be not only practical, hygienic, agreeable, but beautiful also ..."[43] Jeanneret was slightly annoyed by the show where he looked in vain for the conservative, urbanist ideas of his previous role model, Camillo Sitte, and the latter's "picturesque town planning". Instead, given their preference for monumental projects and geometrical axes, he accused Hegemann and the rest of "absolutist town planning".[44] The *Étude* shows that Jeanneret did not immediately embrace such ideas, but the exhibition for the first time brought him into contact with the rationalist urbanism of the twentieth century.

By contrast, Jeanneret enthused wholeheartedly for one of the other exhibitions at the Congress, the "Clay, Cement and Limestone Industry Exhibition" assembled by Peter Behrens. Jeanneret visited it for the first time on Sunday, 12 June, and for a second time on Thursday, 16 June. While in the *Étude* he hardly discusses the exhibition in detail, his diary offers much more:

I discovered some very interesting things behind the hodge-podge impression that such an exhibition always makes. Above all, there are completely new foundations here for architecture and interior design. The new materials will require different shapes and other forms of decoration. ... All kinds of cladding and plaster are on show, very beautiful, very durable, and they can be dyed in numerous ways ... Moreover, there is an increased use of cement to make artificial stone. Here we can see something that seriously casts into question our principles of what is authentic and sincere. Be that as it may, the materials made in this way are very beautiful. They need to be given shapes

43 Quoted on p. 171.
44 See Werner Oechslin, introduction to Albert E. Brinckmann, *Deutsche Stadtbaukunst in der Vergangenheit* (1921), repr. Vieweg, Brunswick, 1985, pp. 5 ff.

that reflect their origins. ... All of this demonstrates how hygiene is making inroads into construction ... the trend towards monolithic structures, the disappearance of the love of frilled woodwork and wood in general, replaced by materials that are plastic (i.e. they can be moulded), not flammable, washable and can be disinfected ...[45]

This clarifies something Jeanneret only alludes to in the *Étude*: in the exhibition, Jeanneret saw the basis for a completely new, fundamental, architectural vocabulary,[46] an impression intensified by the accompanying lectures. The lecture on "Heimatschutz" he mentions in the *Étude* was given by Hermann Muthesius; the other named speaker was Karl Ernst Osthaus. In his address, Osthaus praised the future of building in concrete, emphasising that concrete

allows far greater tension than was possible with any previous material, meaning we may be able to achieve greater spaciousness when applying it. Another possibility that concrete offers is that for multi-storey buildings, the footprint of the upper floors can be designed independent of the ground plan of the lower floors. ... Moreover, concrete is, as you know, tamped in boxes. In other words, it is obvious that we should avoid making it in the profiles to which we are accustomed from carving in stone. Concrete will thus lead to a far more compact design of the shape of buildings.[47]

45 *Le Corbusier, Les voyages d'Allemagne – Carnets*, op. cit., Carnet II, pp. 99–193.
46 The exhibition no doubt contributed decisively to Jeanneret's championing white plaster facades, which were to become a key hallmark of his buildings. In Munich, he had earlier seen the white facade of the Villa Brakl and judged it positively, and a few weeks later, while in Mittenwald, he wrote: "We should oblige all inhabitants of my houses to have a lime pit behind their houses so that they can replaster their houses once a year." While at this time Jeanneret's buildings had dark facades, the one he designed next, the villa for his parents in La Chaux-de-Fonds in 1912, was whitewashed: it was called the *Maison Blanche*.
47 Karl Ernst Osthaus, "Material und Stil", lecture at the Third Annual General Meeting of the German Werkbund, 10–12 June 1910. Quoted from Rainer Stamm, ed., *Karl Ernst Osthaus, Reden und Schriften*, Walter König, Cologne, 2002. Oechslin (1987) has pointed out that here Osthaus preempts the free ground plan (*plan libre*) that Le Corbusier published in 1927 as one of the "Five Points for a New Architecture".

When Osthaus proclaimed in his lecture that iron "has in certain respects today already been overtaken by concrete, by freestanding walls and other inventions,"[48] Jeanneret noted in his diary that "Muthesius protested against the claim that iron is dead, speaking of bridges that are very beautiful; the other responded that concrete is better."[49] However, the speakers concurred that new materials would mean that architects had to redefine how they addressed the forms of buildings. Just as in the past materials were given their commensurate forms, new materials needed to develop their own immanent aesthetics and not be shaped in keeping with traditional design principles. In other words, notions of preserving buildings of historical merit and an architectural culture needed to be construed not purely as maintaining aesthetic criteria, but should follow the logic of being commensurate with the materials used. Thus all the speakers advocated ideas that were far more progressive than the conservative principles

Emile Cardinaux, poster for an exhibition about "Heimatschutz" in La Chaux-de-Fonds, 1909, BV

of "Heimatschutz" espoused by Paul Schulze-Naumburg, views which until then Jeanneret had shared.[50] Osthaus's lecture even anticipates Jeanneret's *plan libre*.

Jeanneret dedicated the following section to another exhibition, the "Exhibition of Painted Rooms". He saw it twice in Germany, in 1910 in Munich and in 1911 in Hamburg. While he strongly attacked the presentation in Munich, he praised the presentation in Hamburg. He used the discrepancy between the

48 Ibid.
49 *Le Corbusier, Les voyages d'Allemagne – Carnets*, op. cit., Carnet 1, p. 21.
50 See Paul Schulze-Naumburg, *Kulturarbeiten*, 9 vols, Callwey, Munich, 1901–17. With this publication and his initiation of the "Heimatschutzbund", Schultze-Naumburg not only laid the foundations for a holistic philosophy of architecture with nationalist, conservative traits, he was also, as the founder of the Saalecker Werkstätten, an important advocate of the applied arts movement. In the 1930s he wrote propaganda on Nazi design ideals.

two versions as an occasion to make some general remarks on exhibitions in Germany *per se*. Exhibitions had already become major society events, starting with the Great Exhibition at the Crystal Palace in London in 1851 and followed by many other major exhibitions of a similar kind. The bourgeoisie had adopted such events as a favourite leisure pastime; specifically, the presentation of the applied arts appealed to various different interests among the public who attended them. They laid claim to being art, provided down-to-earth ideas for people's own homes and, with their close links to industry, kindled a fascination in technological innovation, something that always attracted a large audience in the nineteenth century, which so loved technical progress. This fact was exploited by the progressive representatives of the applied arts movement, who used it in the form of countless exhibitions to attract the attention of the public. The popularity of the "artists" troubled more traditional representatives of the applied arts, since with interiors becoming ever more matter-of-fact, entire professions such as decorative painting were doomed to die out. The conflict is highlighted in a passage in *Innendekoration* of 1909:

These purported opponents are the "artists", against whom the feeling among those involved in the apartment scene is as fiercely bitter as it is incomprehensible to outsiders. "Artists" are said, by having invented the "modern style", to have intervened irresponsibly in things relating to commerce and the crafts trades and to have damaged business *per se*. They have made the public troubled, doubting and discerning. Their expensive furniture is too plain and their "machine furniture" too cheap. They cannot be excused the fact that their exhibitions and publications are such crowd-pullers that so much attention is caught by modern apartment art while the craftsman is bypassed, if not spoken of only in terms of being backward.[51]

51 See *Innendekoration*, vol. XX, September 1909, n.p.

Conservative artistic craftsmen organised exhibitions of their own to preserve their importance as an independent trade. Jeanneret commented on this wooing of the public and buyers in a paragraph on the "Exhibition of Painted Rooms". This had been arranged in Munich from a traditional viewpoint by the representatives of the guilds. By contrast, in Hamburg it was curated by Director Meyer of the Hamburg College of Applied Arts and included well-known representatives of the applied arts movement such as Bruno Paul and the Vereinigte Werkstätten. With his preference for the more modern presentation, Jeanneret was not only in line with public opinion of the day, but also with that expressed by the trade press, as shown by another article from *Innendekoration* in 1910:

> Last year's exhibition by the decorative painters was a failure because the organisers tried to show nice and clean imitations of wood grains, marble textures and the like. Such things were no longer included in this year's exhibition, and thus the level achieved gives grounds for hope for the future, even if it was still not agreeable. And it would certainly not be a problem if the decorative painters were again to function as assistants to the artists creating the rooms. But they must free themselves more of that one-sided mindset that only considers the "décor" and nothing but décor, and concern themselves not just with a piece of ornamentation or plaster vine and instead consider the room as a whole which they are to instil with a colourist tone and mood.[52]

EN ROUTE TO INDUSTRIAL DESIGN

In the *Étude*, the discussion of the applied arts exhibitions is followed by several sections in which Jeanneret focuses on companies and products from the new applied arts

52 See "Ausstellung Bemalter Wohnräume", unsigned commentary, in *Innendekoration*, August 1910, n.p.

movement. In the field of furniture, the Vereinigte Werkstätten für Kunst im Handwerk had been established in Munich as early as 1899: the founding members included Bruno Paul, Berhard Pankok, Hermann Obrist, Richard Riemerschmid and Peter Behrens. They had achieved international fame with their work at the Paris World Exposition in 1900. In 1901, the Dresdner Werkstätten was set up, founded by Karl Schmidt, himself a trained cabinetmaker: it was devoted from the outset to a reduced line of simple furniture and standardised and series production. In 1906–7, Schmidt persuaded Wolf Dohrn, still a young man, to come to Hellerau and organise the Hellerau Garden City, where the production plant for the Dresdner Werkstätten was to be placed in a fitting environment. In 1907, the Vereinigte Werkstätten and the Dresdner Werkstätten agreed to join together to form the Deutsche Werkstätten. However, it soon became clear that the two enterprises were too different to allow for a fruitful merger. While the Vereinigte Werkstätten insisted on artistic furniture, often in the Art Nouveau vein and not always commercially viable, the Dresdner Werkstätten prioritised simple, standardised products from the beginning, and these were also a great business success. The nascent conflict between the two partners was highlighted in Jeanneret's diary notes dating from his visit to the Deutsche Werkstätten in Munich in April 1911:

Visited Schimon, Director of the Deutsche Werkstätten on Thursday, 19 April, in order to obtain information from him on the company and the store at Odeonsplatz. Deutsche Werkstätten GmbH is not a joint stock corporation, but consists of shares owned by several interested parties, bankers and others. Karl Bertsch and Director Schmidt themselves hold significant shares. Vereinigte Werkstätten für Handwerkskunst, Aktiengesellschaft – these two firms are currently united. However, they will soon be parting company again. That has already happened in Berlin.[53]

---

53 *Le Corbusier, Les voyages d'Allemagne – Carnets*, op. cit., Carnet IV, pp. 18–19.

Jeanneret was less interested in the internal problems and more in the production and aesthetics of the new furniture industry, on which he gathered information during his visit:

> I then toured the workshops with Schimon: there are 100 workers and employees, whereas there are 600 in Dresden. These two factories do not together constitute a whole, but have two different administrations. The workshops are housed in very dilapidated buildings, one stuck next to the other. ... This shows that, compared with the palace in Hellerau, you can get something going even with very little.[54]

The "palace" in Hellerau was designed by Richard Riemerschmid and production started there in 1910. In October 1910 Jeanneret saw the freshly commissioned building with its rustic look for the first time: he was not especially impressed by the outside. But the latest technical equipment, which he describes in the *Étude*, was something he recorded in his diary: "There are vacuums for the dust, as follows: one machine in the cellars, and pipes as if for central heating to which a rubber hose is connected when there is cleaning to be done."[55] He was also fascinated by the production of furniture in series: "As soon as an order comes in from one of the branches in Berlin, Munich, etc. the artist is instructed to prepare a drawing; the plan is then sent to the orders office in Hellerau, which registers it and distributes each category of object to the respective production section: embroidery, metalwork, cabinetmaking, etc."[56] The network of Deutsche Werkstätten branches referred to here included Hamburg, Hanover, Bremen, Berlin and Cologne. Jeanneret visited the Munich branch in April 1910 and the Berlin branch in June 1910; the latter did not really impress him. In March 1911 he again went to the Deutsche Werkstätten in Berlin, and the

54 Ibid., p. 20.
55 Ibid., p. 37.
56 Ibid., Carnet III, p. 54.

The paint shop at the Dresdner Werkstätten in Hellerau, Dresden, c. 1910

Richard Riemerschmid, building for the Deutsche Werkstätten in Hellerau, Dresden, 1909–10. Overall view

following month to the Bremen branch. Here he reached the conclusion presented in the *Étude*: "that the whole arrangement from top to bottom is made with perfect taste, whether by Bertsch in Munich or by Paul in Berlin and in Bremen. ... The conception is unified, the effect irresistible."[57]

Development of the AEG logo, 1905–08

Jeanneret was similarly fascinated by the uniformity and rigour of the new "industrial art" at AEG, which he described in the next passage in the *Étude*.[58] Founded in 1883 by Emil Rathenau, the company was renamed Allgemeine Elektricitäts-Gesellschaft four years later. Over the next 25 years, the company grew at astonishing speed, from 6 to 32,000 employees. Between 1908 and 1911–12 (just when Jeanneret was in Berlin and several new AEG factories were being built), the payroll doubled again to reach over 70,000. In the early years, AEG's corporate architecture was designed by Franz Schwechten, followed from about 1896 until about 1906 by Alfred Messel. By 1906 Messel was increasingly focusing his energy on planning Berlin's Museum Island, and AEG looked for a successor who was capable of designing both the architecture and the face of its products. Between 1906 and 1907, Building Councillor and Director of the AEG factories Paul Jordan decided to bring Behrens on board. At that time, Behrens had designed few buildings other than his own house in the artists' colony on the Mathildenhöhe in Darmstadt in 1900, a few temporary structures at expositions in Turin, St Louis and Cologne, and about half a dozen smaller buildings in cities in western Germany. After periods in Munich and Darmstadt, he was at the time Director of the College of Applied Arts in Düsseldorf and had made

57 Quoted on p. 175.
58 For extensive information on AEG's corporate history and Peter Behrens's work for the company, see Tilmann Buddensieg, *Industriekultur, Peter Behrens und die AEG, 1907–1914*, Mann, Berlin, 1979.

a name for himself above all with the pavilion for the Del-menhorster Anker-Linoleumwerke at the Dresden Applied Arts Show in 1906 and with the accompanying corporate printed matter for AEG.[59] On 28 July 1907, the cooperation between Behrens and AEG was officially announced in the *Berliner Tageblatt*. On 30 August, the same newspaper carried an essay in which Behrens presented his radically matter-of-fact programme for AEG entitled "Art in Technology":

> Now, today's trend shall henceforth be followed, which entails machine-based manufacturing not imitating handicrafts with other materials and historical stylistic currents, but instead assuring as close a link between art and technology as possible. Namely, by emphasising and exactly executing mechanical production with an artistic thrust and thus arriving at forms that are innate and unique to the machine and mass production and are similar in substance to it. … The intention must now be to create types for such products and achieve a cleanly constructed graceful beauty for them that is consistent with the materials used. … Since all products of society are more or less closely related to architecture, the intention is of general significance, to the extent that the spatial artists and architects will be able to allocate the objects which formerly, owing to their technical character, would have been irritants in the artistic structure of space, to an artistic slot in the overall order.[60]

In his general remarks on Behrens and AEG, Jeanneret seemed to take his cue from this and possibly also from one of the many other texts on Behrens and AEG published around 1910 by journalists such as Joseph August Lux, Karl Ernst Osthaus and Karl Scheffler. However, Jeanneret collected the decisive information for the section on Behrens and AEG himself when he attended the Werkbund

Joseph August Lux, *Ingenieur-Aesthetik*, title page, 1910

---

59 Buddensieg suggests that the similarity between the Anchor Pavilion of 1906 and the AEG Pavilion Behrens had already designed for the Berlin Shipbuilding Show indicates that the Anchor Pavilion prompted AEG to employ the services of Behrens. See Buddensieg, ibid., pp. 11–20.
60 Peter Behrens, *Kunst in der Technik*, in *Berliner Tageblatt*, 29 August 1907, quoted from Buddensieg, *Industriekultur*, ibid., p. 274.

Peter Behrens, AEG assembly hall at Hussitenstrasse, Berlin, 1913

Peter Behrens, AEG showroom at Ackerstrasse 71–76, Berlin, c. 1910.
Jeanneret visited and described the showroom on 10 June 1910

Congress in Berlin in 1910. In his diary, he painstakingly recorded all the details of a tour of the AEG factories in Berlin's Wedding district on 10 June 1910. The tour started with a product presentation in the Ackerstrasse building:

In the exhibition room we were shown all the lamp models, above all the arc lamps, different models, which are juxtaposed to the old type that is covered in curlicues and a harsh black lacquer. The shapes and above all the apparatus necessary for an installation (contact switches, buttons, meters, dynamos etc. etc.) are reduced to the simplest possible version. As simple cast-iron sheet metal, their entire beauty stems from their proportions and the material used. These strict forms full of generous dimensioning are above all impressive rather than beautiful or different, they are in fact neutral. ... We are then taken into the upper part of the factory, where 6,000 men and women are employed as workers, the next factory will have 8,000, and AEG employs in total 36,000 workers. ... Then on to the turbine hall. A large facade designed by Behrens and full of character. ... The machine is running, the men just prepare the work piece and then have the machine convey it.[61]

Peter Behrens, arc-lamp for AEG, 1907

For all his enthusiasm, Jeanneret was not uncritical in his assessment of Behrens, as can be seen from an observation he made on the General Town Planning Exhibition that same week. In the "Old Berlin" section chair designs by Schinkel were on show, which reminded him of the neo-classicism in Behrens's furniture designs, "even if Behrens does not achieve the charm and quality craftsmanship of the earlier furniture, which is so indebted to a great tradition."[62] Nevertheless, he applied to work for Behrens and started as a draftsman in his studio in Neubabelsberg on 1 November 1910.[63] The relationship between the two was not particularly good. After waiting so long for Behrens to agree to employ him, Jeanneret was then hardly able to find anything right about

61 *Le Corbusier, Les voyages d'Allemagne – Carnets*, op. cit., pp. 42–50.
62 Ibid.

his work. He wrote that Behrens was chronically overworked, criticised his authoritarian treatment of staff and complained that he hardly made friends with anyone in the office and that most of his colleagues were better dressed than he was.[64] Not until the turn of 1911 did Jeanneret start to attribute his difficulties to his own lack of prior knowledge. This change of heart is documented in a letter to L'Eplattenier dated 16 January: "The shock of joining Behrens was brutal. … I arrived there without any idea of what constitutes a style and completely without any knowledge of the art of profiles and their harmonious relationship. I assure you it is not easy. And nevertheless these are the relationships that bring forth the harmonious forms. … Behrens insists strictly on rhythm, subtle proportions and so many other things of which I was completely unaware."[65] What we can infer from this persisted during the course of 1911: the closer he came to the end of his employment on 1 April, the more he considered his time in Behrens's office to be an invaluable apprenticeship. In May 1911, in Berlin for the last time, Jeanneret already saw the city and his time with Behrens in a softer light. On 25 November 1911, working on the final version of the Étude after returning to Switzerland, Jeanneret wrote to William Ritter: "I shed tears for Munich and almost for Behrens."[66]

63 During his time at Behrens's studio, Jeanneret initially rented a room at Stahnsdorfer Strasse 83 in Neubabelsberg, very close to the office; at the end of November he moved to another small room directly next door at no. 81, in the Riedels' apartment. Behrens's office was a kind of interim stop-off for many well-known contemporaries, including Mies van der Rohe and Walter Gropius, who had left the office earlier in 1910. Gropius left to work on the Fagus-Werken; Mies to plan the Perls House.
64 Letter to William Ritter, 12 December 1910, FLC.
65 Letter to L'Eplattenier, 16 January 1911, FLC.
66 Letter to William Ritter, 25 November 1911, FLC.
67 *Le Corbusier, Les voyages d'Allemagne – Carnets*, Carnet IV, pp. 58–61.

BOOKS, GOODS AND
THE "ART OF PRESENTATION"

At first sight it may seem strange that Jeanneret dedicated the next section to the reform of book art and the newly emerging "art of presentation". But in his later books Jeanneret tended to combine the promotion of industrial goods with his activity in book design, and he was no doubt strongly influenced to take this approach by what he learned in Germany. He knowledgeably lists the brothers Karl and Wilhelm Klingspor, Walter Thiemann, Emil Rudolf Weiss and Fritz Helmuth Ehmcke as the key advocates of "modern" graphics in Germany, and also does not forget to point to Peter Behrens's work in this field. Advertisements by German typographers, among others, were to be found in the yearbooks of the Werkbund, to which they also were committed. Between 8 and 19 April 1911 in Munich Jeanneret jotted down the names of Thiemann and Behrens as typographers; on 24 April he recorded a visit to the Klingspor brothers in Offenbach:

→ Plate X

Hans Rudi Erdt, poster for Opel, 1911

> The very friendly director explained the company's development to me. … The beginnings were difficult, all manner of research, resistance among the public, then the workers. All the type came from England and above all from America. Klingspor says he exchanged over 300 letters with Behrens before the Behrens Antiqua font was ready.[67]

A few days later in Düsseldorf he met Ehmcke, head of the specialist Printed Art class at the College of Applied Arts. What Jeanneret fails to mention in the *Étude* but reports in his diary is the collaboration between Peter Behrens and his wife Lili in the field of book design. Above all, Lili Behrens designed endpapers for books. Jeanneret wrote on her elaborate marbling technique:

> Mrs Lili Behrens makes book endpapers for luxury editions. The highly artistic technique I witnessed in Weimar is used here with exquisite liberty and

Alfred Messel, Wertheim department store, Leipziger Strasse, Berlin,
before the opening, 1904. View into the atrium

imagination, turning each of these large-sized sheets into a poem. The technique gives rise to a mixture of meandering lines, with flowers or other clear motifs. Another new resource worthy of discovery.[68]

However, on balance, book design and typography play a subordinate role in Jeanneret's own diary entries. Only where they are related to architecture in the form of so-called "presentation art" is his interest fired. The presence of advertising in German cities triggered countless discussions on how the emerging industrial culture should appropriately be represented in the urban fabric. Historical photographs show Berlin to have been inundated with billboards on the walls of buildings.

Charles-Édouard Jeanneret, design for Paul Ditisheim's department store, La Chaux-de-Fonds, 1913

At the same time, some of Europe's largest department stores were being built there, such as Kaufhaus Wertheim, which Jeanneret enthusiastically studied. He gathered other ideas for the presentation of goods in Hagen when visiting Karl Ernst Osthaus in May 1911. Stimulated by Berlin, where as early as September 1909 a shop-window competition with famous designers such as Endell and Behrens had caused a stir, Osthaus had organised a similar event in Hagen and also a touring exhibition by the Deutsches Museum für Kunst in Handel und Gewerbe. During Jeanneret's visit, Osthaus no doubt also mentioned the ideas he was to publish two years later in the second Werkbund yearbook on the topic of "The Shop Window":

The new window should be matter-of-fact. Each article does not want to tell a story, but to be itself. The display should be a display, a compilation that does not seem bound together by "literary" ties. The dress is an article, not the skin of an expectantly listening beauty made of wax. This presumes a change in all notions. This is to turn our backs on Romanticism, applied to the shop window. It is but an accompanying phenomenon of the great

68 Ibid., Carnet III, pp. 88–9.

change that in architecture rejected historical styles, refuted painted decoration on the stage, and has its organ of economic policy in the form of the Deutscher Werkbund.[69]

Osthaus's idea of a "matter-of-fact" shop window in which the goods only embodied themselves was in line with the Werkbund's stance and the effort to stand apart from the opulent presentations of the nineteenth century. But the *Étude* shows that for him the art of presentation was always also an art of seduction, fully cognisant with illusionist effects. We can already sense here his fetishisation of the modern commodity world, which he was to pursue ever more strongly in the 1920s in the context of *L'Esprit Nouveau*:

To attract the client with the seduction of comfort, of luxury, of beauty, to open its doors to the crowds that surge in, to display beautiful materials in excessive detail, that is to say, to put them in the hands of the onlooker so that he receives some physical impression, a sensual contact, to intoxicate him, and to tempt him – that is the new tactic of the merchant. Astonishingly tasteful window displays in the most intense centres of life arrest the hurried crowds. The doors are actually heavenly portals. There are free elevators; the complete neutrality of the salesmen never makes one feel pressured. But, so that this often fantastic display in immense Halls flooded with light never becomes wearisome as in an Oriental bazaar, it needed an order, an organisation, a rhythm, a feeling for colour; the exploitation of decorative resources inherent to merchandise needed tact, taste – style if you will – **the art of display**.[70]

69 Karl Ernst Osthaus, "Das Schaufenster", *Die Kunst in Industrie und Handel*, Jahrbuch des Deutschen Werkbundes, Jena 1913, pp. 59–69, quoted from Stamm, *Karl Ernst Osthaus, Reden und Schriften*, op. cit., pp. 86–91.
70 Quoted on p. 179.

THE "DEMOCRATISATION
OF THE SINGLE-FAMILY HOUSE "

With his choice of title for the next section, "Art in the Service of Speculation", Jeanneret makes reference to a fundamental conflict in the entire idea of garden cities, and proceeds to discuss it. Since the mid-nineteenth century, the notion had been propagated of residential estates providing living space for a growing industrial proletariat at affordable prices and in surroundings close to nature. The movement's breakthrough came with the book *To-Morrow* written by Ebenezer Howard in 1898.[71] In its wake, Letchworth Garden City (1903) and Hampstead Garden Suburb (1907) were both founded outside London, combining all the elements of independent towns, grouped around a central park and surrounded by a broad green belt. In Germany, the Werkbund, the Bund Deutscher Bodenreformer, the Bund für Heimatschutz, the cooperative movement and the Deutsche Gartenstadtgesellschaft (founded in 1902 by landscape gardener Hans Kampffmeyer) advocated the idea of garden cities. In 1909, Jeanneret, on a trip to Paris, used the opportunity to cross the Channel to visit Hampstead and Letchworth. In Germany, he was now able to observe how the idea of the garden city went beyond creating individual colonies and became a key idea driving urban planning. However, this trend also meant that the garden city became a fashion that was taken up by property developers in order to market estates in the growing German suburbs which no longer had much in common with the original garden city ideals. Yet, despite this

Charles-Édouard Jeanneret, drawing of Hampstead Garden Suburb, London, for the planned publication "La construction des villes", 1910. FLC

71 Ebenezer Howard, *To-Morrow: A Peaceful Path to Real Reform*, Swan Sonnenschein, London, 1898. New editions published after 1902 were entitled *Garden Cities of To-Morrow*.

Charles-Édouard Jeanneret, photograph of a workers' estate near Stuttgart, April 1910

Hermann Muthesius, row of single-family houses, "Am Dorffrieden"
in Hellerau Garden City, 1911–2

trend, which Jeanneret addressed in his slightly sarcastic chapter heading, his fascination for the garden city prevailed.

In La Chaux-de-Fonds, Jeanneret had been attracted to socialist ideas through the journalist Carlo Picard, a friend of the family, and the latter's journal *La Sentinelle*. Shortly after departing for Germany on 15 May 1910, Jeanneret wrote an article, "L'Art et l'Utilité Publique", for the essentially bourgeois newspaper in La Chaux-de-Fonds, *National Suisse*, describing a housing estate outside Stuttgart initiated by a "society of the prosperous on behalf of the wellbeing of the working class" which he had studied en route to Munich.[72] In Munich, he came upon an example of the garden city in the nascent suburb of Waldfriedhof, and recorded his impressions in his diary in the form of several sketches and notes. He was able to study other examples in Berlin in June 1910. There, or so he wrote in the *Étude*, the General Urban Planning Exhibition showed "truly revolutionary trends": "The streets will be like the avenues of parks; they will curve for the best utilisation of the terrain. The stations will be charming in their fitness, and the large green spaces jealously guarded."[73] Following the exhibition, Jeanneret also toured the Berlin suburbs of Zehlendorf, Frohnau and Neubabelsberg, and on departing from Berlin on 21 June he wrote to William Ritter: "While Vienna has grown in concentric rings, Berlin has gone one better, opting for radial lines and thus enabling entire forests to penetrate right to the heart of the city."[74] In May 1911, he visited another garden city project, the artists' colony initiated by Karl Ernst Osthaus in Hohenhagen. There, in 1906, Osthaus had acquired a large swathe of land for which Peter Behrens drafted the development plan. By the

72 Charles-Édouard Jeanneret, "L'Art et l'Utilité Publique" in *L'Abeille*, supplement to *National Suisse*, 15 May 1910.
73 Quoted on p. 182.
74 Letter to William Ritter, 21 June 1910. FLC.

time Jeanneret visited, the estate included Osthaus's own home by Henry van de Velde, three villas designed by Behrens and eleven buildings by J. L. Mathieu Lauweriks.[75]

He gained the most important insights into the garden city when touring Hellerau, near Dresden. There, in the preceding years, the first and to this day most significant garden city in Germany had arisen. The founder of the Dresdner Werkstätten, Karl Schmidt, had transformed numerous individual plots acquired from local farmers into one coherent piece of land; on 4 July 1908, he founded the Gartenstadt-Gesellschaft Hellerau, commissioning Richard Riemerschmid to devise the development plan. The goal was to establish a cooperatively structured garden city, containing not only the Dresdner Werkstätten production facilities but also the homes of the workers, and where members of the educated middle classes who were sympathetic to the objectives of the estate could also acquire houses. Two house types were presented at the 1908 Munich Applied Arts Show in order to attract future inhabitants. In 1909, work had started erecting the first buildings; in March 1910 the first inhabitants had moved in, and in 1913 Hellerau already contained over 385 homes. Wolf Dohrn, employed as manager by Schmidt in 1906, outlined ideas in a treatise of 1908 that were astonishingly similar to those put forward by Jeanneret in the *Étude*:

Advertising poster for houses by Hermann Muthesius in Hellerau, c. 1910

75 Osthaus wrote on this: "Sale of the plots was subject to the condition that the buildings' design be solely in the hands of this artist. The unusual nature of this intention prompted many a contradiction; however, since then, following my own residence, the Hohenhof, which van de Velde built from 1906–8, now three other villas made by Behrens have arisen, and 11 by Lauweriks, whose inhabitants are evidently happy with the preferential feel of the grounds being given a consistent face." *Karl Ernst Osthaus, "Lebenslauf", in Stamm, op. cit., pp. 23–6.*
76 *Die Gartenstadt Hellerau – Ein Bericht von Wolf Dohrn*, Diederichs, Jena, 1908, repr. in Wolf Dohrn, *Die Gartenstadt Hellerau und weitere Schriften*, Hellerau-Verlag, Dresden, 1992, p. 10.
77 Quoted on p. 181. Jeanneret's emphasis.

In Germany and England, approximately at the same time, the idea arose of using planned estates to create better and cheaper apartments. Better: thanks to the rational overall layout of the estate. Cheaper: by avoiding the speculation that pushes land prices up. ... While garden cities have to date been more considered as fulfilling an economic and social task, here they have also received due architectural recognition... the land is "not permitted for offer, purchase, sale or encumbrance on the open market, and cannot become an object of speculation like some stock-market security; instead it has to belong to the totality of those who as a community occupy the land ..."[76]

Even if, unlike Dohrn, Jeanneret essentially emphasised the English origins of the garden city, he agreed with the former's view about the original idea: "Today in Germany it needs to be beautiful **as a whole**; it needs to be harmonious, built in a unique style and precisely in that style and with that ease which have become so successful among the very rich classes."[77]

Jeanneret stayed in Hellerau on various occasions, mainly because his brother Albert had moved there in 1910. Albert had trained as a violinist, and  the dance teacher Émile Jaques-Dalcroze from Geneva asked

Rhythmic gymnastics according to Émile Jaques-Dalcroze

Stage production by Émile Jaques-Dalcroze, c. 1900

Marcel Duchamp, *Nude Descending a Staircase*, 1912. Oil on canvas,
Louise and Walter Arensberg Collection, Philadelphia Museum of Art

him to accompany him to Hellerau to set up a rhythm school, in which Dalcroze intended to teach his new views on the subject. The school was to be based in a Festival Hall designed by Heinrich Tessenow, which first opened its doors in the winter of 1911. During his second visit to Dresden at Christmas 1910, Jeanneret was offered a part in the project by Tessenow while it was still under construction, but Jeanneret declined as he was not given enough say in it. Dalcroze's lessons were a great success in Hellerau. While the first course, held in winter 1910 in provisional rooms, attracted only students, the number had rocketed to 495 pupils just three years later.[78] Hellerau became a centre of modern stage art, and in the years that followed attracted artists such as Mary Wigman and Isadora Duncan, convincing Jeanneret to investigate more closely the subject of rhythm. An enthusiastic concert and theatre goer himself, he felt it was not just a question of music or theatre but had to become part of modern society. While still in Germany, Jeanneret jotted in his diary the title of a publication, "Rhythmus in der Arbeit", recommended by Leipzig professor Johann Friedrich Schär, which probably refers to *Arbeit und Rhythmus* (1896) by Karl Bücher. In the 1920s in *L'Esprit Nouveau* he wrote an article saying that the rhythm of the human body must via industrial labour be transposed on to the industrial product and thus on to the entire designer environment.[79] The Hellerau garden city as a "social *gesamtkunstwerk*" provided Jeanneret with the first example of a setting in which such an intensive link between man, architecture and a modern environment could be tried and tested.

→ **Plate VIII**

Charles-Édouard Jeanneret, title page of the article "La Rythmique" in *L'Esprit Nouveau*, **numbers 2 and 3, 1920**

[78] See Manfred Sack, "Schönere Häuser, bessere Menschen" in *Die Zeit*, 27 July 2006, p. 80.
[79] Le Corbusier, "La Rhythmique" in *L'Esprit Nouveau,* numbers 2 and 3, 1920.

ACADEMIC AMBITIONS

The German art colleges were, ever since Art Nouveau, a driving force behind the German reform movement. This was already evident in Muthesius's polarising lecture of 1907 to the Berlin Handelhochschule, during which he stated that the conservative "representatives of the applied arts, the factory owners and dealers, have protested vociferously against the new movement and its backers, the Applied Arts Show in Dresden and the applied art colleges."[80] Gradually, alongside the traditional colleges in the applied arts museums, new colleges had been founded, offering instruction in tune with the requirements of industrial production. For Jeanneret, there was nothing new about the zest for innovation shown in the education system: he himself had studied on the newly created course at the Nouvelle Section in La Chaux-de-Fonds. The dovetailing of training and practical work was already practised there and had played some part in the first building design work Jeanneret was commissioned to do. It was thus only logical that in the concluding part of the *Étude* he dedicated a separate section entirely to training in the applied arts, a decision also necessary in the light of how the book project itself had evolved. After all, the text had been commissioned by those responsible for the art college in La Chaux-de-Fonds specifically in order to identify role models for modernising instruction in this field in Switzerland. During his trips, Jeanneret dutifully filled out page after page of his notebooks with observations that ranged from teaching methods via working atmosphere and cleanliness to the students and the teaching staff.

80 Hermann Muthesius, "Die Bedeutung des Kunstgewerbes" lecture at the Berlin Commerce College, quoted from Junghanns, *Der Deutsche Werkbund*, op. cit., pp. 139–40.

Jeanneret's first visit of this kind took place on 17 June 1910 in Berlin, when he went to the teaching institute of the Royal Museum of Applied Arts, whose director was Bruno Paul. Jeanneret mentioned Paul's house in the gardens of the college and praised the training, which had strong links to practical work enabling students actually to undertake contract jobs.[81] When travelling back to Berlin, Jeanneret intended to visit the Art Academy in Weimar on 22 June, which Henry van de Velde had founded in 1906. However, van de Velde was away and Jeanneret's diary reveals that he felt ambivalent about the academy: "To my mind, this college seems to be asleep, as it again relies on the principle of paid masters who spend the whole day doing nothing. Prohibition to work in line with nature. Van de Velde has kept teaching on pure ornamentation for himself, the other fields are covered by specialised masters who compose things together with the students, but van de Velde exercises a corrective hand throughout."[82] Jeanneret was only positive as regards the academy's aims, which were to take up the local Saxon crafts traditions, infuse its products with new life by opting for more modern shapes and thus give the local trades and the students' training an edge. After Weimar, Jeanneret moved on to visit the University of Jena, which did not have an art academy but was interesting as a building – it had been built in 1903–8 by Theodor Fischer. Jeanneret postponed most of his visits to colleges of applied art until his second tour at the end of his stay in Germany

German Bestelmeyer, extension wing to Munich's Ludwig Maximilian University, 1906–10. Jeanneret visited the building several times and mentioned it appreciatively in his diary

in April–May 1911. In Munich in April 1911, he visited Wilhelm von Debschitz's "Teaching and Experimental Laboratory", then travelled to Stuttgart to visit the art academy

81 Le Corbusier, Les voyages d'Allemagne – Carnets, op. cit., Carnet I, p. 30.
82 Ibid., Carnet II, pp. 146–47.

there under Director Bernhard Pankok. He records in his diary that he felt a certain unease with Pankok's opinions and at the same time passed a more general judgement on the experiences he had had of the German colleges:

> Here, the tendency is more to train artistic workers than working artists. Pankok's influence is to be felt. I feel the good man is stuck in sixteenth-century Gothic, and his approach is overly pedantic. … The projects give me the feeling that in this college, as in all the others, nothing rises above the mediocre.[83]

After brief visits to Karlsruhe, Heidelberg, Frankfurt and Hanau, Jeanneret travelled on to Darmstadt, where he had almost nothing but scorn for the Mathildenhöhe artists' colony and above all for Joseph Maria Olbrich. After travelling up the Rhine to Cologne by boat, he paid a visit to the Düsseldorf College of the Applied Arts and its director, Wilhelm Kreis. Having only recently criticised the latter's Bismarck Tower in Dresden, Jeanneret was pleasantly surprised when he encountered the man's modern teaching methods, finding them "more meaningful than I would have expected from Kreis".[84] From Düsseldorf, he travelled on via Hagen to Hamburg, where on Friday, 12 May 1911, he was received by Director Meyer of the local applied arts college. As in Düsseldorf, here he ascertained that almost all the professors were younger than forty and his general assessment was decidedly positive. Alongside an openness for contract jobs and joint initiatives, he was also fascinated by the novel teaching methods, including above all work with cut-out silhouettes in primary colours, because "when cutting them out one can only express oneself through the contours, and that spawns the style, the rhythm and the synthesis".[85] The last applied arts college he visited, on 23 May, was the Royal

---

83 Ibid., p. 35.
84 Ibid., Carnet IV, p. 69.
85 Ibid., Carnet IV, p. 26.

Exhibition of works by students of Charles-Édouard Jeanneret
in the Post Office, La Chaux-de-Fonds, 1913

67

Academy of Applied Arts in Dresden, which he roundly criticised, writing that it taught in an "ancient and stupid manner" and in all fields all that was to be seen was "poor taste" and "cold tradition".[86]

It goes without saying that such assessments crop up in the *Étude* only in a diluted form, as Jeanneret's research work in Germany was generally valued for its positive case studies. Thus his commentaries can also be read as an ideal agenda for the advancement of his own art academy in La Chaux-de-Fonds: he emphasised that almost all colleges published elaborate prospectuses, almost all of them had modest beginnings, but nevertheless would undergo radical change "because the authorities have felt the profound influence that the new teaching in the applied arts has had on industry and commerce, as well as on the cultural advancement of the nation."[87] Not least, Jeanneret owed it to L'Eplattenier to provide a concluding section in a motivated vein, featuring actual proposals for improvements that had already been tried out, since the latter had procured him the stipend that enabled him to write the *Étude*. It was also in line with Jeanneret's own

Charles-Édouard Jeanneret, design for a brochure for the *Nouvelle Section*, c. 1912. FLC

future plans: after his return to Switzerland, he started work as a lecturer at the Art Academy in La Chaux-de-Fonds and endeavoured to realise some of the ideas he had been exposed to in Germany. Thus he exhibited student projects in the local post office and supported brochures that were designed to document the academy's progressive thrust. Moreover, he advocated creating a counterpart to the Werkbund in French-speaking Switzerland, to be called *L'Œuvre* – it was duly founded in 1913.[88]

86 Ibid., p. 37.
87 Quoted on p. 200.
88 See on this Brooks, *Le Corbusier's Formative Years*, op. cit., p. 354.

BETWEEN BOURGEOISIE AND BOHEMIANISM

Although Jeanneret concerned himself with his own activities alongside work in his own newly established architecture office, his travels across half the continent had shown him all too clearly how confined life in his home canton was, and this prevented him from fitting snugly back into his old ways. Immediately on arriving back in Switzerland, in November 1911 he wrote to Auguste Perret:

> It was the burial, the death of my youth. On the morning of my return I went up to Pouillerel, and beyond the deep Doubs Valley France spread out before me into eternity. … L'Eplattenier, my mentor and friend, counted on me. … Standstill, sombre, monotonous, grey, life in the provinces, in the Swiss provinces.[89]

Jeanneret had matured into an adult while travelling, and felt himself ever more constrained in La Chaux-de-Fonds. This impaired his relationship with L'Eplattenier. In fact, the constant

Ceramic vase, purchased by Charles-Édouard Jeanneret between Budapest and Istanbul in 1911, FLC

postponement of production of the *Étude* had already weighed sorely on their friendship, as had Jeanneret's trip to Istanbul which he had undertaken against his teacher's advice. It was thus only a matter of time before the two parted company. This happened only a few months after the *Étude* came out, as Jeanneret wrote to Auguste Klipstein:

> Things are over between me and L'Eplattenier! … Everything fell apart in the space of only six months. … He awaited my arrival impatiently. But when we saw each other, we were both astonished and amazed. Overly different notions of art, and the differences slowly but surely caused all sympathy between us to cease. … Now it is over, the only flower that brought me here, that kept me here.[90]

89 Letter to Auguste Perret of 12 November 1911, quoted from Jenger, *Le Corbusier, Choix de lettres*, op. cit.
90 Letter to Auguste Klipstein of 20 August 1912, ibid., p. 96.

Charles-Édouard Jeanneret on the Acropolis, Athens, 1911

The *Étude sur le mouvement d'art décoratif en Alle-magne* marks this break-up in two respects. On one hand, it is the last document from the time when Jeanneret was a student, dating back to a close link with L'Eplattenier without which the context of Jeanneret's commitment to the art academy of La Chaux-de-Fonds would have been inconceivable. On the other hand, it is already a document of the change in Jeanneret's views which made the break with his teacher inevitable. Looking back, Jeanneret himself always attributed this change less to the influences of

Le Corbusier, illustration from *L'Esprit Nouveau* no. 1, 1920

Germany and more to the subsequent *voyage d'orient*, which he pointed up as having brought a kind of illuminating insight. In reality, however, the contrast between the east and Germany, between German rationalism and Oriental-Mediterranean *joie de vivre* was not as clear as Jeanneret, with his tendency to polarise, would have it. While still in Germany, he had come across studies such as that by Alexandre Cyngria-Vaneyre, whose appeal for an independent architectural vocabulary for the Jura he read while working for Behrens.[91] Without doubt, in the foggy Berlin winter the book must have offered a tempting contrast, shaped by Latin Classicism, a simple response to Jeanneret's search for a Swiss identity of his own.

Late Roman chip carrings from Alois Riegl's *Spätrömische Kunstindustrie*, 1901

However, references to Classicism and the east were not unknown to the German applied arts movement. Alois Riegl's *Spätrömische Kunstindustrie*, a book with which Jeanneret was

---

91 See Alexandre Cingria-Vaneyre, *Les entretiens de la villa du rouet: Essais dialogues sur l'art plastique en Suisse romande*, Jullien, Geneva, 1908. The core of Cyngria-Vaneyre's hypothesis is the statement that the inhabitants could be traced back directly to Greco-Roman origins, having fled in antiquity to the remote valleys of west Switzerland. A rejuvenation of the culture of this region would therefore have to recollect its Greco-Roman traditions and express this in its architecture, too. Cyngria-Vaneyre's in part apocryphal theories repeatedly linked cultural considerations with racist motifs. Jeanneret read the book in November 1910 while working for Behrens.

→ Plate VI + VII

familiar, was of immense importance to the movement,[92] and Wilhelm Worringer's *Abstraktion und Einfühlung*, which was in Jeanneret's pocket during his trip to Istanbul, prompted him to focus closely on so-called "primitive culture" in the context of applied arts. We can also discern the interest the German applied arts movement had in non-European cultures from a lecture by Karl Ernst Osthaus on "Material and Style", which Jeanneret heard at the 1910 Berlin Werkbund Congress and on which he took extensive notes:

Years ago I travelled to North Africa, through Algeria and down into the Sahara. ... Between the fields the huts of the natives stuck out, and all of these huts were made of wickerwork reeds. The railway drew closer to the Atlas, clambered up rocky heights, from which in the course of the Middle Ages the opulent forests of Roman times had been felled. ... The result was that the Kabyles built their huts from stone. These stone houses perfectly resembled those that we can encounter in the European mountains, for example in the high mountains. Then the railway travelled down the other side to the Sahara, and there one glimpsed Bedouin homes, made neither of wickerwork nor of stone. They were tent covers, which they had woven and, made of goat's wool or camel hair, spanned over light rods. The homes had taken on the form predicated by the material.[93]

Jeanneret's interest in folklore and archaic art was also nourished in Germany by several exhibitions, such as the "Ethnographic Exhibition" in the Wertheim department store, which he mentions in the *Étude*:

This permanent exhibition, instituted under the auspices of the "Ethnographic Society", is a sales counter for all of the objects of European popular art. There one buys, at good prices, prestigious Czech, Romanian, Serbian and Bulgarian embroidery, thick Finnish tapestries, sculpted wood from Russia,

---

92 Alois Riegl, *Spätrömische Kunstindustrie*, Verlag der Staatsdruckerei, Vienna, 1901.
93 Karl Ernst Osthaus, "Material und Stil", lecture at the Third Annual General Meeting of the German Werkbund in Berlin, 10–12 June 1910. Quoted from Stamm, *Karl Ernst Osthaus, Reden und Schriften*, op. cit.

pottery from all of Germany, from Bohemia, from Thoune, etc. and also Negro and Japanese basketry, etc. This is not merely a display of bric-a-brac but a selection of the finest examples.[94]

All these examples show that the German applied arts movement could not be reduced, as Jeanneret reduced it, to a purely rational movement that took its cue from industry and was in part a hegemonic movement. We can explain Jeanneret's clear and insistent juxtaposition of a strict Teutonic Germany with a sensuous east in the light of his decided tendency to exaggerate, which was to become more pronounced in later years. In Germany, Jeanneret probably recognised so many aspects of his own character that they virtually provoked the twenty-year-old to challenge them. Jeanneret's "German side" is blatantly obvious: his mother, a piano teacher, had sent him to a kindergarten managed in line with Friedrich August Fröbel's reform teaching principles[95] and had always attached great importance to her sons' musical training. In Germany, he hardly missed an opportunity to attend a concert or opera, and repeatedly praised the works of German composers such as Gustav Mahler, Johann Strauss and Richard Wagner. Various diary entries attest to his familiarity with a "typically German" culture of middle-class domesticity, for example when he describes the afternoons of family music played in Theodor Fischer's home in Munich, and also to his thoughts on the idyll of an imaginary garden city that he felt was demonstrated by the General Town Planning Exhibition. In Jeanneret's life, phases of euphoria forever alternated with melancholic, depressive moments in which the German *tourments gotiques*[96] were far closer to his heart than

94 Quoted on p. 173.
95 See Brooks, *Le Corbusier's Formative Years*, op. cit., p. 10.
96 *Le Corbusier, Les voyages d'Allemagne – Carnets*, op. cit.

he liked to admit. This can be seen from his self-portrait from the *voyage d'orient*:

> I open them wide, my short-sighted eyes behind my glasses – these sad glasses that give the impression of my being a doctor or a "clergyman". I utter far too many stupid things. Unfortunately I on occasion change my mind, much to the annoyance of those close to me, and I contradict myself more than is tolerable. And so it happens that on days in which I am in a bad mood I rage, while at other times, my inquisitive Demoiselles, I feel deeply moved when I pass through a dreamland to the rhythm of exuberant scherzos that as a whole are dominated by great harmony.[97]

Charles-Édouard Jeanneret, study for a pattern with pine motifs, 1911, FLC

Here, Jeanneret paints a picture of moods that oscillate between isolation and ostentation, evoking another of his German role models, Friedrich Nietzsche, whose *Thus Spake Zarathustra* he had read in Paris as early as 1908. We can see that it prompted him in crucial ways to point himself up as the solitary *Übermensch* and artist in search of the truth. On a Christmas card he sent his parents in 1909, Jeanneret portrayed himself as a crow on a mountain.[98] The mountain, as the home of the prophet Zarathustra in Nietzsche's work, was something with which Jeanneret was intimately familiar, and the crow, the *courbeau*, was later to provide the cue for his pseudonym of Le Corbusier. A fundamental principle of the solitary artist and thinker was to reject anything that seemed obvious; without doubt this contributed decisively to Jeanneret's classification of Germany in the *Étude*, which borders on the cliché.

---

97 Le Corbusier, *Le voyage d'Orient*, Forces Vives, Paris, 1966, quoted from *Le Corbusier, Viaggio in Oriente*, op. cit., p. 13.
98 See on this Charles Jencks, *Le Corbusier and the Continuous Revolution in Architecture*, Monacelli Press, New York, 2000, p. 54.

FROM CLASSICISM TO THE
TRACÉS RÉGULATEURS

For all his inner resistance, Jeanneret's experiences in
Germany were to inform all aspects of his work in the years
that followed. Many German architects started out as painters, thus proving to Jeanneret that there need be no contradiction between working as an artist and an architect. He
enthusiastically recorded this in the *Étude*, too:

→ **Plates VII + VIII**

> Men devoted to matters of art abandon the brush and concentrate their
> efforts on architecture: Peter Behrens, the painter from Munich and Darm-
> stadt, becomes the director of the department of architecture in Düsseldorf,
> then advisor to the AEG. ... Bruno Paul, caricaturist for Simplicissimus, is
> appointed director of the school of Berlin (architecture and decorative art);
> Bernard Pankok, painter, is director of the school in Stuttgart (interior archi-
> tecture and decorative art); Wilhelm Debschitz, painter, creates a new school
> of decorative art and interior architecture.[99]

So how was the inspiration Jeanneret found in Germany
reflected in his architecture? Specifically, when attending the
Werkbund Congress in June 1910, he encountered a radical
counter-model to the traditionalist notion of architecture
espoused by L'Eplattenier. When travelling to Berlin he
admired the medieval German cities, but after his visit he was
full of praise for the Classicism of the Sanssouci Palace in
Potsdam, and also for the recourse to elements of Biedermeier
that were popular around 1910 among architects such as
Bruno Paul and Peter Behrens. A few months later he con-
fessed his "conversion" to Charles L'Eplattenier:

---

99 Quoted on p. 150 f. After visiting Muthesius, Paul and Behrens in Berlin, on
27 June 1910, Jeanneret wrote to Charles L'Eplattenier: "Would you believe that no
one and nowhere am I believed that I am an architect; everyone believes I have the
qualities of a painter."

Oh, but I nevertheless have you to thank for the enlightenment, those Stauffer, that they tore me from my medieval silt and showed me the most amazing of styles. … Versailles. … The Classical clarity. However, it took long for me to fully liberate myself of all the medieval pettinesses that caused me to see art on such a very small scale.[100]

Peter Behrens, Elektra boathouse, 1912

That same autumn, Jeanneret had to contend painfully with the fact that the new architectural notions were only realisable with very sound craftsmanship, which he learned when working for Peter Behrens. Behrens expected his staff to have a command of a doctrine of proportions that Jeanneret had not yet mastered and had to learn with great effort. The first project in which he was confronted with Behrens's careful search for harmonious proportions was the Elektra boathouse which he worked on. Other Behrens buildings that Jeanneret studied during his travels reinforced this insight. These included Behrens's own house in Darmstadt, dating from 1899 (an early work indebted to Art Nouveau, which Jeanneret pardoned him for), as well as the Cuno and Schröder houses in Hagen (1908–9) and the crematorium in Hagen-Delstern (1907). In his doctrine of proportions, Behrens, among other things, drew on the thinking of August Thiersch and his book *Proportionen in der Architektur*, published in 1883, in which Thiersch advocated above all the rhythmic consistency of design elements in facades and ground plans.[101] The key focus was less on the actual structure of the building and instead on its effect on the viewer.

Jeanneret initially criticised as superficial such a focus on the visual impact of outer harmony, yet in his own buildings designed after returning to Switzerland there is no ignoring this influence of Behrens.[102] On seeing Behrens's crematorium in Hagen, Jeanneret jotted down an idea he had for a house

100 Letter to L'Eplattenier, 16 January 1911, FLC.
101 August Thiersch: *Die Proportionen in der Architektur*, Diehl, Darmstadt, 1883.

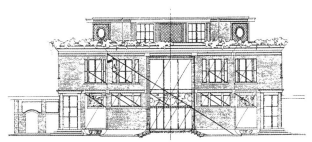

CONSTRUCTION RÉCENTE D'UNE VILLA

Peter Behrens, Cuno and Schöder houses, Hagen, 1908/09

Villa Schwob with added proportional lines *(tracés régulateurs)*, illustration by
Charles-Édouard Jeanneret in *L'Esprit Nouveau* no. 5, 1921

he was already planning for his parents: "if one stands at the threshold to Behrens's crematorium, the six pillars that bear the load of the building leave a very noble impression, taken together with the countryside (the pillars are made of black cyanite, perhaps for the living room)."[103] Behrens's influence is especially noticeable in Jeanneret's Villa Favre-Jacot created in 1912, the ground plan of which reveals parallels to Behrens's Cuno House, as Francesco Passanti has demonstrated, and the facade of which is reminiscent of the neo-Biedermeier style evidenced at that time by many villas in Berlin and Munich, not to mention Schinkel's gardener's house for Sanssouci in Potsdam. Yet where Jeanneret did indeed discern positive qualities in German architecture, he usually explained them by saying they revealed a French influence. This can be seen from a diary entry on the Villa Stuck, alluding eclectically to Italian villas: "Behrens denies what the art of his country possesses in terms of German qualities. Bruno Paul, Troost purport to be French. If the German element is really to be beautiful it first sheds all of its Nibelung-like memories."[104]

Even after the Villa Favre-Jacot, the mark made by Germany on Jeanneret remained visible in his buildings. Although references to historical styles now took a back seat, in the concept for the 1915 Maison Dom-ino and for the

Charles-Édouard Jeanneret, sketch for a *Maison Dom-ino*, 1915

1916 Villa Schwob there is strong evidence of Jeanneret's borrowings from industrial construction and the debate on "typification", both of which he had

102 For an exhaustive study of the proportional relations between buildings by Jeanneret, Behrens and Schinkel, see Francesco Passanti, "Architecture: Proportion, Classicism and other Issues", in Stanislaus von Moos, Arthur Rüegg, eds., *Le Corbusier before Le Corbusier*, Yale University Press, New Haven/London, 2002, pp. 69–97.
103 *Le Corbusier, Les voyages d'Allemagne – Carnets*, op. cit., Carnet IV, p. 72.
104 *Ibid.*, pp. 134–5.

encountered in Germany. The introduction of an industrial aesthetics and the related processes were to remain a central focus of his work. In 1918 he joined up with the company Everit to try to make industrial semi-finished products from cement asbestos; in 1920, for a brief period, he collaborated with a tile factory in Alfortville. He had also not forgotten Behrens's doctrine of proportions, as can be seen in 1923 when he published his *tracés régulateurs* and thus a theory of proportions of his own, which would have been inconceivable without the stimulus of Behrens's method. But instead of mentioning Behrens, Jeanneret preferred to cite the French architectural tradition, adopting the concept of *tracés régulateurs* from French architectural historian Auguste Choisy.[105]

FROM GARDEN CITY TO *VILLE RADIEUSE*

The Berlin Werkbund Congress in 1910 triggered a change in Jeanneret's notions of urbanism similar to those of architecture. In this field, Jeanneret's ideas prior to his trip to Germany were strongly influenced by his teacher L'Eplattenier, who was in turn a disciple of Camillo Sitte's concepts of "painterly town planning".[106] Jeanneret read cities fully in Sitte's terms, photographing the soft curve of roads and picturesque groups of houses, and collecting postcards displaying medieval sights. Yet such a view became untenable, at the latest after he attended the German Town Planning Exhibition in Berlin. Above all, the highly diverse variations on garden cities and workers' housing estates showed Jeanneret

105 See Le Corbusier-Saugnier (pseud.), "Les tracés régulateurs", in *L'Esprit Nouveau* no. 5, February 1921, pp. 563–72. The text was later included in *Vers une architecture*.
106 See Camillo Sitte, *Der Städtebau nach seinen künstlerischen Grundsätzen*, Graeser, Vienna, 1889.

that the tasks of urbanism could not lie in rejecting the challenges of the Industrial Age but instead in proactively tackling them. Even the monumental projects in the exhibition section dedicated to the "Greater Berlin" competition, although he was essentially sceptical of them in the *Étude*, no doubt in part persuaded him to shift position, as they encouraged him to think on a "greater scale" himself.[107]

In 1914, Jeanneret had the opportunity to plan a garden city himself in La Chaux-de-Fonds. He was enthusiastic in a letter to his mentor Auguste Perret in Paris:

> I have been assured of the 120 houses which I told you about, the agreement will be signed after my return on the following basis: that I will be sole architect of the garden city if I manage to get the communal authorities to accept the allotment plan I have devised.[108]

Charles-Édouard Jeanneret, study for a garden city, 1914. FLC

Jeanneret was not able to convince the authorities, however, and the plan was never realised. Yet perhaps that was only logical. The plan he presented on behalf of his client Arnold Beck, with its rustic buildings, was reminiscent of the garden city in Hellerau with buildings designed by Riemerschmid, Muthesius and Tessenow. Such a project would hardly have withstood his own judgement for longer than a few years: his urbanistic theories progressed so swiftly that in 1915 he completely abandoned work on his essay "La construction des villes" because he no longer shared the book's underlying idea, which followed in the wake of Sitte. In 1922 he proposed the *Ville contemporaine pour 3 millions d'habitants*, one of the most radical town-planning utopias of the twentieth century. Instead of

---

107 He was supported in this view by Karl Ernst Osthaus, who in his lecture mentioned that no city came close to having the qualities of Paris and its planning in the Haussmann idiom. See Gresleri, ed., *Le Corbusier, Voyage d'Orient – Carnets*, op. cit., Carnet I, p. 12.
108 Letter to Auguste Perret, 1 July 1914, quoted from Jenger, *Le Corbusier, Choix de lettres*, op. cit., p. 108.

softly curving roads, the contemporary city was dominated by huge overhead roads; gabled houses had given way to gigantic residential towers that stretched to the heavens. Yet, however radical this looks at first sight, again there is no avoiding the evidence of the ideas of German reformist architecture. To have nature penetrate the city remained the key Corbusian idea. In the next stages in the development of his urban planning projects – from *Plan Voisin* (1925) via the *Ville Radieuse* (1928) through to the master plan for Chandigarh – it gained ever greater importance. And the fact is that Jeanneret continued to have the thrust of German housing estates in mind, if on a smaller scale, as can be seen from his housing estate for workers designed for entrepreneur Henri Frugès in 1925 in Pessac, which in many respects is reminiscent of the workers' estates in Stuttgart, Berlin and Hellerau.

FROM MACHINE FURNITURE TO *OBJET TYPE*

In the field of applied arts, the ideas that Jeanneret confronted in Germany were also diametrically opposed to his prior views. While L'Eplattenier had conveyed to his pupil the anti-industrial, elitist notions of John Ruskin and William Morris, in Germany Jeanneret was exposed to what we could today term the emergence of industrial design. As of 1900 in Germany, designs by renowned *auteurs* were for the first time produced on a mass scale. In 1905 Richard Riemerschmid designed a series of "machine furniture" for the Dresdner Werkstätten with which Jeanneret was as familiar as he was with Bruno Paul's

Richard Riemerschmid, chair ("machine furniture") for the Dresdner Werkstätten, 1905

1908 type furniture for the Vereinigte Werkstätten. During his travels in Germany, Jeanneret visited all the important German companies and retail houses in the furniture sector, including not only the Deutsche Werkstätten in Dresden and

→ **Plate XII**

Munich, but also furniture houses such as the Hohenzollern-Haus and Keller & Reimer in Berlin, and Ballin in Munich. His visits there gave him the opportunity to study the latest furniture designs, and he made many sketches in June 1910 at Keller & Reimer in Berlin.[109] Details of furniture created by Alfred Grenander and Albin Müller document Jeanneret's special interest in movable cantilevers, individual technical parts and mechanical functions; they are strongly reflected in his design for a bureau for his mother a few years later.

However, Jeanneret was still sceptical of an exclusively mechanical approach to furniture, and this was to remain the case. He adhered to the Classicist vein longer as regards furniture than he did in architecture, feeling that "style" played a key role in furniture and industrialisation was merely an instrument that should not be allowed to define the style. The ambiguity between furniture as machine and the search for "style" is also the key factor influencing his efforts at designing furniture in the period after the *Étude*. For example, the bureau for his mother featured rounded arcs reminiscent of a garden *loggia* in a Palladian villa. His 1915 furniture designs

Charles-Édouard Jeanneret, chair for Hermann Ditisheim's apartment, 1915

for the Ditisheim family bring to mind Bruno Paul's 1908 type furniture, in which an industrial aesthetic blended with Classicist borrowings. As he increasingly worked as an interior designer, Jeanneret found himself travelling to Paris more often, where he purchased furniture for his wealthy clients in La Chaux-de-Fonds. At this time, he was still thinking about German furniture design, as is testified in a letter to Auguste Perret of 1913 in which he comments on Leon Werth's publication *Meubles modernes* and writes about the sketches by Francis Jourdain contained in it, saying "people did stuff like that in Germany ten years ago".[110]

---

109 *Le Corbusier, Les voyages d'Allemagne – Carnets*, op. cit., Carnet I, pp. 84–91.

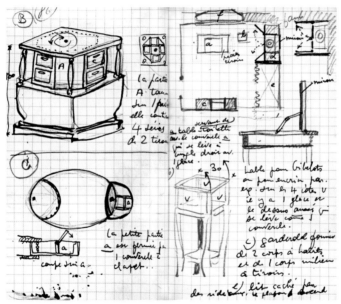

Albin Müller, interior design for a lady's room in the
Keller & Reimer furniture store, Berlin, 1910

Charles-Édouard Jeanneret, diary sketches of furniture by Albin Müller
and Alfred Grenander in the Keller & Reimer furniture store, Berlin, June 1910

Jeanneret did not just discover the first industrially manufactured "auteur" items in Germany, but also other objects – above all, the world of innovative products whose very existence often became conceivable only with the advent of modern technology and which thus lacked typological predecessors. Jeanneret was quite taken with such products as early as his guided tour of AEG in June 1910; on another occasion, he noted in his diary "very beautiful porcelain pissoirs".[111] Unlike furniture that had arisen as a result of centuries-old genealogies, with such objects there could be no question of style, only the issue of how specific design and production standards could be developed. This was also the basis of the so-called Werkbund dispute on the concept of "typification", with Henry van de Velde on one side and Hermann Muthesius on the other. The debate was not aired publicly

Photograph from the Werkbund yearbook _Der Verkehr_, 1914

until the 1914 Werkbund exhibition in Cologne, but during Jeanneret's visit to Germany in 1910–11 different opinions were afloat among members of the Werkbund on the relationship between industry and individuality. Jeanneret shared Muthesius's position that one needed to make use of what industry had to offer instead of returning to hand craftsmanship, the path championed by van de Velde. However, Jeanneret did not understand "typification" the way that Muthesius did, as a set of specifications to be applied to industrial production; he construed it more as an organic process. An object-"type" would thus automatically develop between production requirements and customers' demands, and therefore needed only to be recognized and promoted. Industrial objects could be prime examples, or so Jeanneret felt, but so could objects of popular art whose

110 Letter to Auguste Perret, 7 December 1913, quoted from Jenger, _Le Corbusier, Choix de lettres_, op. cit., p. 103.
111 _Le Corbusier, Voyage d'Orient – Carnets_, op. cit., p. 33.

Cliché Hostache.

MAISONS EN SÉRIE

Illustration "Maisons en série" from *Vers une architecture*, 1923

forms had been optimised through the centuries. Jeanneret mentioned the latter in the *Étude*, when discussing the "Ethnographic Exhibition" in the Wertheim department store, praising the fact that a selection of the "finest examples" had been on show.[112] Another way of studying the development of types in Germany was in the many advertisements in the Werkbund yearbook appendices. There, industrial products were often presented against a white background and in a reduced view to ensure that attention was directed to their basic forms, thus their "type". In the years directly after the *Étude*, Jeanneret repeatedly used such objects in his interiors – either semi-industrial items, such as *bergères à paille*, or collectors' items, which he had purchased on his trip to the east.[113]

→ **Plate X + XI**

The illustrations in the Werkbund yearbook appendices were probably very influential for Jeanneret, not only because of the industrial objects depicted but also because of their clear graphics. They bring to mind the visual idiom Jeanneret represented in *L'Esprit Nouveau*, founded in 1921 together with Amédée Ozenfant and Paul Dermée. The world of images of *L'Esprit Nouveau* included cars, bentwood chairs, planes, pissoirs, pipes, steamships and many other objects typical of the Industrial Age. Often they were presented against a white background or in unexpected contexts, as they frequently served as a way of emphasising typological qualities.

Jeanneret's understanding of the "type" still differed from the various German interpretations of the concept, as can be seen from his controversy with Walter Gropius, who with the Bauhaus propagated a search for underlying geometrical forms of industrial design. In *L'Esprit Nouveau* in 1923, Jeanneret rebuked Gropius for the fact that in Germany and at

---

112 Quoted on p. 173.
113 See on this Arthur Rüegg, "Marcel Levaillant and 'La question du mobilier'" in von Moos, Rüegg, eds., *Le Corbusier before Le Corbusier*, op. cit., pp. 109–31.

86

Photograph of the steamship *Cecilie* with the New York skyline behind,
from the Werkbund yearbook *Der Verkehr*, 1914

Photograph of the grain silo in Montreal from the Werkbund yearbook, 1913,
retouched by Le Corbusier for *L'Esprit Nouveau* no. 1, 1920

the Bauhaus overly abstract standards were imposed, whereas they should instead evolve from production and experience. That said, the ideas that prompted Jeanneret's own view of *objets types* had also mainly originated in Germany.

FROM THE *ÉTUDE* TO *L'ESPRIT NOUVEAU*

→ **Plate XIV + XV**

Jeanneret collected many of his articles for *L'Esprit Nouveau* and a few years later published them in four books: *Vers une architecture* (1923), *Urbanisme* (1925), *L'Art décoratif d'aujourd'hui* (1925) and *La peinture moderne* (1925).[114] In these publications he presented summaries, in the form of handy propaganda treatises, of his new dogmas in the fields of architecture, town planning, the applied arts and painting. At first sight, these have little in common with the *Étude*: the stilted language in the *Étude* has given way to a telegram-like style, the layout of the books is modern and geared to the images, and the feel of the books brings to mind the collaged pictures created by the artistic avant-garde, frequently oscillating between Surrealism and slapstick. Yet these later books are more closely related to the *Étude* than appearance would suggest. This is most obvious in the case of *L'Art décoratif d'aujourd'hui*, owing to the thematic links. Many of the thoughts expressed there can be traced back to the *Étude*, including those on popular art, on the significance of industrial production, on the emerging bourgeoisie's desire to imitate, not to mention the influence of machine-based production in general on the design of industrial goods. Yet, as regards design, points of contact with the *Étude* can also be

---

114 All these books were published by Editions Crès in Paris. They largely consist of essays that Le Corbusier had previously published in *L'Esprit Nouveau*, in part under pseudonyms.

identified in the other three books. The typography of the *Étude* shows that Jeanneret was already endeavouring to provide a vibrant layout, one in which we can sense his later, freer use of typography in the 1920s. And even though the *Étude* made no use of images, the books from the 1920s present many pictures testifying to the fact that Jeanneret's stays in Germany opened his mind to a new world of images. The magazine Innendekoration reported as early as 1909 extensively on Bruno Paul's interior design for the ocean liner George Washington, although it was not taken up by the Werkbund yearbook until

DES YEUX QUI NE VOIENT PAS...

LES PAQUEBOTS

Le Corbusier, title page of an article in *L'Esprit Nouveau no. 8, May* 1921

1913 in an article entitled "Der Verkehr" (Transportation), which bears a strong similarity to Jeanneret's discussion, "Les Paquebots", in *L'Esprit Nouveau*.[115] Jeanneret liked to consult the Werkbund yearbooks as a welcome source of images, as we know from a famous episode in which he had Walter Gropius send him the photograph of a grain silo from the 1913 Werkbund yearbook in order to use it himself ten years later (albeit in a retouched version) in *Vers une architecture*.[116] This episode says a lot about Jeanneret's attitude towards Germany, as did the *Étude*. His time in Germany provided him with a wealth of ideas, which he proceeded to adapt and reshape:

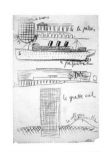

Le Corbusier, illustration for *Précisions sur un état présent de l'architecture et de l'urbanisme*, 1930. FLC

the often overly theoretical notions of the Werkbund were reinvented in the spirit of the artistic avant-garde of the 1920s, infused with a streak of Surrealism such that he often found it easy to sell them as the opposite of German positions, even though they were hardly removed from them.

115 S. R. Breuer, "Der George Washington" in *Innendekoration*, vol. XX, October, 1909, n.p. The illustrations to this article strongly resemble the images Le Corbusier used in *Vers une architecture* and *L'Art décoratif d'aujourd'hui*.
116 See Walter Gropius, "Handel und Verkehr" in *Die Kunst in Industrie und Handel*, Jahrbuch des Deutschen Werkbundes, Diederichs, Jena, 1913 and Le Corbusier, *Vers une Architecture*, Paris, Crès, 1923.

"END OF THE SECESSION"

The final considerations in the *Étude* and the period after its publication show how this tendency in the 1920s evolved. At the end of the *Étude*, Jeanneret criticises the successful Germany of the applied arts (that *allemagne merveilleuse*) saying that there, art seemed to him to be being used more as a vehicle, as an excuse, whereas in its pure form it was now to be found only in France. The "secessionist fire" in Germany had, he submitted, been put out, and artists were in despair at the sheer size of the tasks they faced. Jeanneret prophesied that the country would revert to imitating French examples after one or two years. We can attribute his conclusion not only to his deep-seated scepticism of Germany, but also to his perspicacious feeling for the trend that was to occur in the Werkbund in the years after the *Étude*. The closer the First World War came and the more tension in Europe increased, the closer the links between the Werkbund and the Prussian state became, and the more the idealist outlook of the early years was buried under a nationalist and conservative cloak. When war broke out in 1914, the Werkbund finally pinned its colours firmly to the government's mast; for example, in 1915 it dedicated its yearbook to the design in times of war.[117]

The Werkbund was already in the throes of this change during the Cologne exhibition of 1914, to which Jeanneret was invited as a guest of honour thanks to the *Étude*. He mentioned this, not without pride, in a letter to Auguste Perret in Paris: "The small book I wrote has been such a success that I have been invited here as a guest of honour!!"[118]

---

117 Peter Jessen, *Deutsche Form im Kriegsjahr*, Jahrbuch des Deutschen Werk-bundes, Bruckmann, Munich, 1915.
118 Letter to Auguste Perret, 1 July 1914, quoted from Jenger, *Le Corbusier, Choix de lettres*, op. cit., p. 107 f.

However, he continued by expressing sharp criticism, as if he wished to confirm the prophecy in the epilogue to the Étude: "In all this impressive and to date unique presentation by the Werkbund, what we see is a lot of superficiality and self-complacency!"[119] The theatre of Henry van de Velde especially incensed him – he had already mocked its "exaggerations" in the *Étude*.[120]

Fritz Helmuth Ehmcke, poster for the Werkbund exhibition, Cologne, 1914

Directly after Jeanneret's trip to Cologne, tension between Germany and France reached a peak. Jeanneret's letter to Auguste Perret from Cologne of 1 July was still relatively objective in his criticism of the Werkbund, but his next letter, dated 14 August when the German army was already marching on Paris, was drenched in the nationalist rhetoric of war. Jeanneret's resentment of Germany, which we can sense in the *Étude*, now exploded in the form of tirades against the "eternal enemy":

They have sallied forth, and their brothers, too, into the Holy Crusade? … For us, from west Switzerland, we have been bristling with anger since the end of July and all my friends, officers and soldiers alike, have headed for the border, to support you with enthusiasm and a hatred of them who have kindled too many different, countless and deep-seated aversions in each and every one of us. … Anyone not playing mad and puffing out their chest is no man, is not a dignified being!! On this topic I do not wish to refrain from sending you an article on your monument that I wrote last year. It was used against me, as we are inundated with German-speaking Swiss. Switzerland today is divided. Oh how I wish that a powerful gesture by France would put paid to this Barbarian hysteria![121]

119 Ibid.
120 Quoted on p. 150.
121 Letter to Auguste Perret, 14 August 1914, FLC. The article mentioned, sharply critical of a German war memorial, is Charles-Édouard Jeanneret's "Lettres des voyage. Le monument à la bataille des peuples", in *La Feuille d'Avis de La Chaux-de-Fonds*, 1–4 July 1913.

Walter Gropius, factory building and offices for the Deutz gas engine factory,
at the Werkbund exhibition in Cologne, 1914

Henry van de Velde, theatre for the Werkbund exhibition, Cologne, 1914

This passage makes it abundantly clear how deep Jeanneret's aversion to Germany ran, something that could only be expressed between the lines in the *Étude*. It did not change in the years that followed. In 1919, he even planned a publication, "France ou Allemagne?", in which he intended to point up the difference between the two countries and present it as a matter of principle. Walter Gropius and the Bauhaus brought Jeanneret back to Germany in the 1920s. At the behest of Gropius, Le Corbusier was represented by several projects at the "International Architecture" exhibition during Bauhaus Week in 1923: the *Ville contemporaine pour 3 millions d'habitants* (1922), the *Immeubles-Villas* (1922) and the *Citrohan series houses* (1921). Le Corbusier graciously reviewed the exhibition and his own contributions favourably in the next issue of *L'Esprit Nouveau*, but was not able to forgo the opportunity to highlight the differences between himself and Gropius on fundamental issues. In 1924, he finally published a tirade on Germany under the pseudonym Paul Boulard entitled "Allemagne …" in *L'Esprit Nouveau* – he treated Behrens, Schmitz and others as one, sharply criticised Olbrich, termed the Werkbund an "economic-artistic invasion project", before closing with the damning summary: "Germany has not progressed one step in the question of architecture."[122]

It is all the more astonishing, then, that the Werkbund invited Le Corbusier to the exhibition "The Apartment" only two years later; he enthusiastically seized the opportunity to attend. Conversely, he was now the only architect whom the Stuttgart municipal authorities vetoed, because as a citizen of west Switzerland he was considered French and thus an "eternal enemy". The artistic director of the Weissenhof Estate,

---

[122] Paul Boulard (pseud. of Le Corbusier), "Allemagne …" in *L'Esprit Nouveau*, November, 1924, n.p. Cf. on this also Oechslin, op. cit., p. 33.

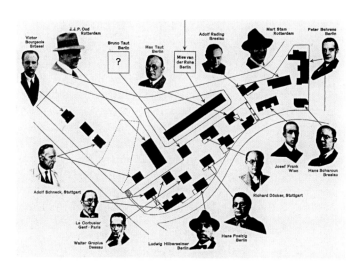

Illustration with site plan and the architects involved from the flyer, for the
Werkbund exhibition "The Apartment", Stuttgart, 1927

Advertising photograph for Mercedes-Benz. In the background,
one of the houses built by Le Corbusier and Pierre Jeanneret on the
Weissenhof Estate in Stuttgart, 1926–27

Ludwig Mies van der Rohe, had to push Le Corbusier's involvement through against the will of the city, justifying it by saying that Le Corbusier guaranteed there would be pan-European interest in the exhibition. Mies's hopes were fulfilled: Le Corbusier constructed his first two houses in Germany at the Weissenhof Estate in Stuttgart and claimed the status of secret star of the entire show. These buildings were, however, to remain his only two on German soil, if we discount the *Unité d'Habitation* in Charlottenburg in Berlin, designed in 1956, from which Le Corbusier distanced himself once the designs had been altered by the Berlin Municipal Buildings Council. Charles-Édouard Jeanneret's critical assessment of Germany and the German applied arts in the *Étude* was to prove a self-fulfilling prophecy.

Le Corbusier, *Unité d'Habitation*, Berlin, 1956

LEARNING FROM THE GERMAN MACHINE

— Alex T. Anderson

LEARNING FROM THE GERMAN MACHINE

Germany emerged suddenly, around 1910, as an immense, acquisitive engine of culture. It amassed expertise in all fields of art and design and slowly turned its enormous productive capacity to the development of objects that would insinuate themselves into the everyday life of Europe. This, at least, was how Charles-Édouard Jeanneret, a young Swiss designer drawn to Munich seeking work, interpreted matters in Germany. While waiting for prospects to turn into employment, Jeanneret received a letter from his school in La Chaux-de-Fonds requesting that he learn what he could about this new force. Although not well known, Jeanneret's report to the School of Art, the *Étude sur le mouvement d'art décoratif en Allemagne*, provides an important contribution to our understanding of the early modern movement as it took shape in the capable hands of German artists and industrialists before the First World War.

→ Plate XVI

Jeanneret admits that the subject of the study is vast, too vast to encompass in a brief report. So its 74 pages limit themselves primarily to pertinent details, written in compressed form. Despite its brevity, contemporary readers of the report found it "remarkable".[1] The Commission of the School of Art determined that its findings were significant to the interests of Swiss arts and education, and so it produced 500 copies of the study, sending 450 of them to regional officials, educators, industrialists and the local press. Many of the remaining copies made their way into the hands of interested parties elsewhere in Europe. Although, as Jeanneret's mentor Charles L'Eplattenier lamented later on, the study received

[1] Hector Guimard, for example, referred to it as "The very remarkable report by Mr Jeanneret." See Hector Guimard, letter to Charles L'Eplattenier, 28 March 1914, reproduced in Charles L'Eplattenier et al., *Un Mouvement d'Art à la Chaux-de-Fonds à propos de la Nouvelle Section de l'École d'Art,* Georges Dubois, La Chaux-de-Fonds, 1914, p. 35.

virtually no response from local recipients, it attracted serious attention in France and Germany. According to L'Eplattenier, it:

> provoked commentary in the principal German dailies, and the French and German periodicals and art reviews, *L'Art et les Artistes, L'Art décoratif, L'Art à l'École, La Grande Revue, Art et Décoration, Kunstwart, Dokument des Fortschritts.* Its author received a request from luminaries at the forefront of the decorative art movement for a second edition in Paris, and even until recently constant requests from booksellers in Brussels, Paris, Vienna, etc.[2]

Interest in the study persisted for several years, even during the war, especially in France.[3]

Jeanneret gathered the information for the report from the summer of 1910 through to the autumn of 1911, and submitted it to the commission in January 1912. By the time he arrived in Germany in April 1910, the Deutscher Werkbund had been in operation for three years, Peter Behrens had been working for AEG for about as long (and had recently completed construction of its immediately famous turbine factory). Two summers before, an exhibition in Munich had prompted an impressed – and very concerned – delegation from Paris to invite members of the Vereinigte Werkstätten für Kunst im Handwerk to display their work in France. These same artists were preparing for what was to become a momentous Salon d'Automne exhibition in Paris when Jeanneret began gathering his data. There was much to study and comment upon.

---

2 Ibid.

3 *L'Art de France* reproduced virtually all of it in two volumes during the spring of 1914: *L'Art de France*, April 1914 and May 1914. And the study provided much of the factual material for a long article speculating on post-war reconstruction by Maurice Storez in the *Grande Revue* of October 1915: Maurice Storez, "Que seront l'Architecture et l'Art Decoratif après la Guerre?" *Grande Revue,* October 1915, pp. 492–521. See especially p. 498: "Before embarking on this study, I would like to thank particularly the Swiss Architect, Mr Jeanneret, who made a very well-documented report on this German modern art movement, which he published in 1912 and which a very French publication, *L'Art de France*, reproduced in its editions of April and May 1914."

Paul Wallot, design for the Reichstag Building, Berlin, 1882. Engraving

Group photograph with Werkbund members, 1912.
Front row, left, is Friedrich Naumann, one of the Werkbund founders

In its many details, the study reveals something of the machinations of the German state at a crucial moment in its history, when having consolidated its power and position in Europe it had begun to turn attention inward to the development of its culture and cultural production. German influence expanded rapidly into artistic and commercial domains, and German tastes were beginning to insinuate themselves into the very fabric of European life. The report bestows much admiration on the German initiatives, but it also gives a frank assessment of what many designers and critics outside Germany saw as a grave threat.

While it is merely the subtext of the report, the "German threat" is the central theme of the introductory remarks and final considerations in the study. In these remarks, Jeanneret aims to show that, despite the great progress Germany had shown in the applied arts, it was neither entirely responsible for its successes, nor was it likely to prevail over France. France, after all, could count on its superiority in matters of taste to see it through the intensifying rivalry with Germany. Jeanneret placed the phenomenon of Germany's rapid, almost parasitic, development of the arts in vivid contrast to the deep-rooted, but faltering, tradition of French dominance in matters of taste:

Now here is an aspect of something new and unexpected: France persists in renouncing its painters and sculptors, the Institute condemns and undermines them. But Germany positions itself as a champion of modernism, creating nothing in the domain of the fine arts to prove itself so, but revealing its new tastes through the systematic absorption (purchase) of the works of Parisian painters and sculptors (Courbet, Manet, Cézanne, van Gogh, Matisse, Maillol, etc.) and, on the other hand, revealing itself almost without warning to be colossal in power, in determination and in achievement in the domain of the applied arts.[4]

---

4 Charles-Édouard Jeanneret, *Étude sur le mouvement d'art décoratif en Allemagne*, Haefeli, La Chaux-de-Fonds, 1912. Quoted on p. 148.

Peter Behrens, title page, *Kunstgewerbeblatt,* 1912

This rather jaundiced view of German "progress" in the arts was surprisingly widespread and persistent. Commentators on German design at the time often tempered their assessment of its undeniably favourable developments – and the impressive organisational structures that made them possible – with deprecating comments about German originality or German taste. Given the military posturing of Wilhelmine Germany, it seemed evident that its intentions, even in art, were aggressive rather than creative. Indeed, a vocal French architect, Maurice Storez, writing during the war, saw German advances in artistic production as much more than a commercial threat. Acknowledging that the inundation of Europe with German-made products was well under way, he envisaged the overflow of German imperialism into the cherished domains of art and from there into the everyday lives of French people.[5] He urged that the advance be met with the force of organisation built on the unassailable foundation of French tastes. But, along with this sort of encouragement, even the most vociferous critics of German design in the early 1910s had to admit that it was their compatriots' complacency, more than any other factor, that had allowed Germany to gain the advantage in the arts.

This was not merely a French complaint. It was voiced, for example, by William Lethaby, one of the more eloquent spokesmen of the late Arts and Crafts Movement in England, who echoed Jeanneret in 1915:

> The first thing in the arts which we should learn from Germany is how to appreciate English originality. Up to about twenty years ago there had been a very remarkable development of English art in all kinds. For five or six years, round about the year 1900, the German Government had attached to its Embassy in London an expert architect, Herr Muthesius, who became the historian (in German) of the English free architecture. All the architects who at

5 See Maurice Storez, op. cit., pp. 500–1.

that time did any building were investigated, sorted, tabulated, and, I must say, understood. ... It is equally true or even more true that the German advances in industrial design have been founded on the English arts and crafts. They saw the essence of our best essays in furniture, glass, textiles, printing, and all the rest, and, laying hold on them, coined them into money. ...[6]

The threat of German competition also helps to explain why a regional School of Art in French-speaking Switzerland commissioned Jeanneret's study in the first place. The school aimed to head off German competition for products of Swiss design by emulating German efforts. When L'Eplattenier convinced the directors of the School of Art to commission Jeanneret's study, he was seeking justification for a reform of the school, so it could help make Swiss designers and manufacturers more competitive against foreign advances on French-Swiss tastes. He later explained that

> The "New Section" of the School of Art was founded in 1911 with the goal of establishing, among ourselves, an effective collaboration of art and industry. In this area we have been outpaced for several years by neighbouring countries, as has been evident in the international expositions and, in a manner more directly perceptible, in the unconstrained and unsettling invasion of foreign products on to our soil. Native industry has been compelled to cede place to German industry, and taste – our taste – must submit to the domination of the outer Rhine or to that of Parisian manufacturers – which is humiliating.[7]

As L'Eplattenier discovered in the brief, tumultuous life of the New Section, however, resistance to anything that appeared to emulate "Germanic" organisation was difficult to overcome.

This was as true in a provincial town of Francophone Switzerland as it was in Paris. On one hand, traditional academic structures still preserved enough influence to sustain

---

6 W. R. Lethaby, "Modern German Architecture and what we may learn from it", in *Form in Civilization: Collected Papers on Art and Labour,* 2nd edn, Oxford University Press, London, 1957, p. 81.
7 "Nouvelle Section" de l'École d'Art, "Prospectus", Haefeli, La Chaux-de-Fonds, 1912, p. 3.

Francis Jourdain, interior with interchangeable furniture, 1912–13.
Musée d'Art et d'Histoire, Saint-Denis, Paris

Bruno Paul, dining room for the German applied arts exhibition, Munich, 1908

effective resistance against any change, particularly if it had a foreign savour. On the other, politically liberal, reform-minded French designers could not abide the presence of the state in artistic matters; and this put art reform at a competitive disadvantage. The Kaiser's financial backing and organisational support had made the German decorative arts movement very effective commercially, but – in the eyes of the French – all the more sinister and distasteful.[8]

The great magnitude of the German threat had first come into focus for French designers during the summer of 1908 at the annual arts and crafts exhibition in Munich.[9] The Vereinigte Werkstätten für Kunst im Handwerk, in particular, prepared displays of interiors, furniture and domestic equipment that gained almost universal admiration from art critics. A delegation sent to Munich by the Municipal Council of Paris came away with a dire proclamation: "The commercial defeat which has threatened us for many years is no longer to be feared, indeed, it has already occurred ... We cannot compensate for the advance which Munich has been able to accomplish to our detriment in the industrial domain." Looking forward to what Parisian designers might expect from Germany later on, the picture was even bleaker. "Only in five or six years from now will we see and experience the complete results, when this army of students begins to produce industrially ... The only thing we can try to do with any hope of success is to begin to prepare the future generation to enter into competition with these countries."[10] This task was daunting because the German initiative was so broad, systematic and effective – as Jeanneret's study would show. It included a significant overhaul of the educational system in Germany,

8 See, for example, M. P. Verneuil, "Le Salon d'Automne", in *Art et Décoration*, vol. 28, July–December 1910, pp. 129–60.
9 *Die Ausstellung München 1908*, Bruckmann, Munich, 1908.

particularly in the crafts, as well as the development of amicable relationships among artists and manufacturers. In 1908, it was clear that Munich was merely a harbinger of a much more substantial movement. Art and industry throughout Germany were poised to embark on large-scale collaborative efforts in various regional workshops, and under the much broader purview of the Deutscher Werkbund.

Deutsche Werkbund logo, c. 1907

Apart from facilitating effective product design and manufacturing, the Werkbund introduced innovative marketing techniques, which rapidly spread the appeal of German products throughout Europe. When Jeanneret visited the artists, institutions and schools that constituted the German decorative arts movement in 1910 and 1911, there was nothing anywhere in Europe to match it. Even if foreign critics were demure in their praise for the artistic merits of German design, they had to profess profound appreciation for the organisation of arts education and production in Germany. It was no doubt at least partly true that "German advances in industrial design [were] founded on the English arts and crafts",[11] as Lethaby declared in 1915, and that German tastes benefited from French advances in the arts, as Jeanneret and others proclaimed. Nevertheless, the commercial success of German design followed from uniquely German initiatives and extraordinarily effective organisational and marketing efforts.

The German state played a crucial role in these initiatives. Having consolidated 26 formerly independent political entities under an empire stretching across northern Europe

10 The delegation included, among others, Frantz Jourdain, president of the Salon D'Automne; Victor Prouvé, president of the Union Provinciale des Arts Décoratifs; Senator Charles Couyba and sculptor Rupert Carabin. See Municipal Council of Paris, "Report on the Second Congress of the Union Provinciale des Arts Décoratifs held in Munich [1908]", in *L'Art et les métiers d'art*, January 1919. Quoted in Arlette Barre-Despond and Suzanne Tise, *Jourdain*, Rizzoli, New York, 1991, pp. 111–13.
11 Lethaby, "Modern German Architecture", op. cit.

from France to Russia, the German empire needed to establish a distinct identity for itself. It did so primarily on the basis of middle-class economics and social values.[12] Two important agents of this were an excellent education system – "a superb educational machine", in the words of one historian[13] – and an extremely vibrant, growing industrial sector of the economy. Stimulated and directed by well-trained engineers and technicians, German industry grew faster in the first decade of the twentieth century than in any other area of Europe. As a result of this growth, middle-class manufacturers and financiers experienced remarkably high standards of living. The labouring class also benefited from a rising standard of living bolstered by a generous state welfare policy. The decorative and industrial arts, supported by the state educational system and industry, provided some of the most visible manifestations of middle-class German economic and political success.[14]

→ Plate I

To propel the development of this sector of the German economy, the state actively promoted the absorption of "foreign" influence through careful analysis of the artistic production of its competitors. This was the charge handed to Hermann Muthesius when he took a commission as cultural and technical attaché to the German Embassy in London in 1896. During his time in England, Muthesius published a general study of contemporary English architecture and under-

12 For an account of the broader origins and manifestations of German nationalism in the late nineteenth century, see Hans-Ulrich Wehler, *The German Empire 1871–1918*, trans. Kim Traynor, Berg Publishers, Dover, New Hampshire, 1985, pp. 102–5, 239–40.
13 John M. Roberts, *Europe 1880–1945*, Longmans, Green and Co., London, 1967, pp. 203–4.
14 Jeanneret pointed out in 1912 that the strength of German education and state support for sciences was central to the strength of the decorative arts in Germany. He also asserted that Germans' native abilities in this area were not comparable to those of the French, but that they had succeeded in dominating the decorative arts trade more through organisation and perseverance than through ability. Quoted on pp. 147–53.

DAS
ENGLISCHE HAUS

ENTWICKLUNG, BEDINGUNGEN
ANLAGE, AUFBAU, EINRICHTUNG
UND INNENRAUM

VON
HERMANN MUTHESIUS

IN 3 BÄNDEN

VERLEGT BEI ERNST WASMUTH, G.M.B.H.
BERLIN W. MARGGRAFEN-STRASSE 11

took more specialised studies on religious and domestic architecture. The last, a comprehensive analysis of the English house finally published in 1904, remains the definitive work on the subject. *The English House* provides a thorough account of English domestic architecture, interiors and furnishings, but it also reveals much about the state of artistic culture in contemporary Germany. In the introduction to the study Muthesius made the startling assertion that his native Germany lacked a viable artistic tradition because its people did not live in houses. Its only hope of rising from an abysmal artistic standing among other industrialised nations, he argued, was to develop more intense and productive connections between art and everyday life. This needed to begin at home. "Artistic education is loudly advocated today," he said, "but obviously its only basis can be the privately owned house."[15] Having the opportunity to take control of one's own environment, to furnish it, to exercise artistic sensibilities at will was the only way to develop a German culture sensitive to art.

Hermann Muthesius, title page of *Das Englische Haus*, 1904

English domestic architecture provided a superb demonstration of the point. Muthesius took pains, however, to assert that simply emulating an English style of house building would not stimulate a German artistic movement. English houses could "provide pointers" for the development of German artistic culture, but the modern German house, and by implication all modern German artistic and architectural production, could only be *German*. "The greatest merit of the English house as it stands completed before us," Muthesius declared, "is that it is *English*, that is, it conforms totally to English conditions, embodies totally English ways of life, is totally suited to local climatic and geographical conditions ..."[16] Although

15 Hermann Muthesius, *The English House,* ed. Dennis Sharp, trans. Janet Seligman, Rizzoli, New York, 1987, p. 9.
16 Ibid., p. 11; Muthesius's emphasis.

108

Hermann Muthesius, Muthesius's house in Berlin-Nikolassee, 1906–07.
Jeanneret was invited to a reception for the Werkbund Congress at
Muthesius's house on 12 June 1910

Henry van de Velde, Grand Ducal Saxon Art Academy, Weimar, 1904–11

English domestic architecture and interiors might offer few specifics upon which Germans could model their own designs, they did demonstrate admirable principles to follow: "To face our own conditions squarely and as honestly as the English face theirs today, to adhere to our own artistic tradition as faithfully, to embody our customs and habits in the German house lovingly – these are the lessons we can learn from the English house."[17] Muthesius contended that any artistic manifestation of the age in Germany had to follow these principles.

In an important polemical text, *Style-Architecture and Building-Art*, which he published on his return to Germany in 1902, Muthesius argued that architecture – "the art of daily life"[18] – had to be the "central issue of the new artistic movement" in Germany.[19] Like contemporary English domestic architecture, it could only succeed by aspiring to become a vernacular, middle-class art.[20] "Even here," he said, "reform can only proceed from the small to the large, from the interior to the exterior."[21] He explained that England had managed to dispense with nineteenth-century "abstract formalism" by reforming domestic interiors, which led to "a total revolution in the domestic building art" and thence to a general renewal of architecture.[22] Germany needed to follow the same trajectory, beginning with a straightforward approach to artistic design, not another externally applied style.[23] A modern building-art in Germany could only derive from German conditions

---

17 Ibid.
18 Hermann Muthesius, *Style-Architecture and Building-Art: Transformations of Architecture in the Nineteenth Century and its Present Condition*, trans. Stanford Anderson, The Getty Center for the History of Art and the Humanities, Santa Monica, 1994, p. 98.
19 Ibid., p. 47.
20 Ibid., p. 94.
21 Ibid., p. 96.
22 Ibid.
23 Ibid., p. 97.

and it could arise only as a uniquely *German* art, even if its inspiration came from abroad.

Given these intentions, it is hardly surprising that foreign observers of the decorative arts movement in Germany continually questioned the viability of German taste, reserving their praise for German organisation and production. The real threat, of course, was that these borrowed and reconstituted tastes would insinuate themselves – as German innovations – back into French or English culture. As

Charles Rennie Mackintosh, Hill House, Glasgow, 1902–3

the decorative arts movement gained the support of German industry and the marketing force of the Deutscher Werkbund, as its products infiltrated foreign markets, the threat became increasingly palpable.

When Muthesius wrote *Style-Architecture and Building-Art*, Germany had already begun to establish a strong arts and crafts movement. Initially adopting Arts and Crafts methods of hand production, new crafts schools and commercial workshops (many of which Jeanneret visited and described in the study) developed a vast range of products including anything from postcards to the interiors of large private houses. They quickly found ways, however, to make effective use of machines and mechanised production processes. In 1905, for example, Richard Riemerschmid developed a line of inexpensive, machine-made domestic furnishings for the Werkstätten in Dresden. Bruno Paul introduced a similar line in Munich three years later. Jeanneret was impressed by these and other products, but he marvelled at the workshops in which they took shape, facilities that were partially mechanised, beautifully organised and incredibly clean.[24]

---

24 Quoted on p. 176. Jeanneret also mentions that designers of objects produced in these factories received commissions on their sale. For a more detailed account of the economic motivations of these workshops, see Frederic J. Schwartz, *The Werkbund: Design Theory and Mass Culture before the First World War,* Yale University Press, New Haven, 1996, p. 160.

In addition to cultivating very fruitful individual efforts by designers such as Riemerschmid and Paul, the Werkstätten became particularly adept at developing collaborative productions. At the 1908 exhibition in Munich, the Vereinigte Werkstätten für Kunst im Handwerk, under Paul's leadership, displayed beautifully coordinated room ensembles that demonstrated, especially to foreign visitors, how far German design had come. The retail showrooms of the various Werkstätten, which occupied highly visible sites in major cities throughout Germany, demonstrated the commercial viability of their approach. Visiting several of these in 1910 and 1911, Jeanneret remarked on their "astonishingly tasteful window displays" as well as their beautifully coordinated sales rooms. He declared:

> Parisians can remain sceptical as to taste, on account of the incompatibility of the two races, which seems to be pronounced here, where everything that offers itself to the eyes is in some way the expression of the German soul; but these Parisians, if they do not admire everything, are at least impressed by the harmony, which is undeniable. From the curtains, the fabrics, the furniture, the rugs, the lighting fixtures, the dishes, the curios, everything is born of the same desire finally to realise affinity, proportion, suitability, **kinship**.[25]

August Endell, window display for the Salamander shoe shop, Berlin, published in the Werkbund yearbook, 1913

While Jeanneret marvelled at these displays, he discerned a broader trend evident in the shop windows of everything from booksellers to department stores in Germany. "**The art of display**," he proclaimed, "is a completely new art. ... It is developing with stunning rapidity."[26] Much of the credit for this widespread progress in retail display belonged to the vastly influential Deutscher Werkbund, which had been founded in 1907 to coordinate and promote the production of German artists and industry. Although its immediate aim was to encourage pro-

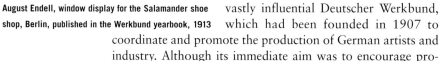

25 Quoted on p. 175; Jeanneret's emphasis.
26 Quoted on p. 179; Jeanneret's emphasis.

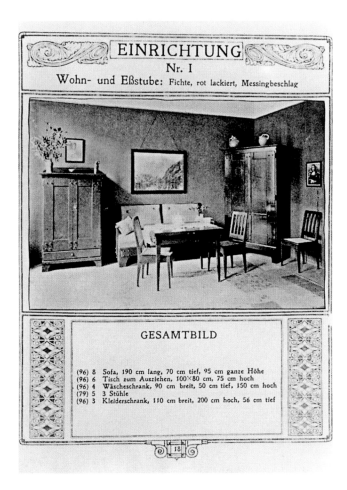

Advertisement for machine-made furniture designed by Richard Riemerschmid
for the Deutsche Werkstätten, Dresden, 1905.
This page illustrates living and dining room furniture in red or blue painted pine

ductive collaboration, the underlying motivation of the Werkbund was to change public sensibilities toward artistic production, from a rather distant and often confused admiration
of "art" to a more straightforward appreciation of quality
and suitability in well-designed objects.

Perhaps the most effective collaboration orchestrated by
the Werkbund was between the Allgemeine Elektricitäts-
Gesellschaft (AEG) and the painter Peter Behrens.[27] The work
Behrens did for the firm provided a remarkable demonstration
of the potential breadth of Werkbund influence. Behrens
designed an amazing variety of objects for the company,
including letterheads, electrical consumer products, workers'
housing and factory buildings. Jeanneret, who worked in
Behrens's office from November 1910 to April 1911, remarked that "not one visible aspect of the building construction or
the production coming out of AEG has not been reworked by
him."[28] But Behrens's influence went well beyond the design of

Peter Behrens, electric kettles for AEG, 1909

objects. His well-known turbine factory of
1909, for example, introduced an altered industrial working
environment that emphasised the benefits of light and space on
the health of workers and the quality of their production.[29] His
efforts also helped to improve the home life of middle-class
consumers in Germany. Thanks to its huge capital reserves,
AEG was able to develop and market inexpensive but well-
built lamps, kettles, sewing machines, fans, etc. – useful items
that had formerly been prohibitively expensive for most

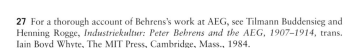

---

27 For a thorough account of Behrens's work at AEG, see Tilmann Buddensieg and
Henning Rogge, *Industriekultur: Peter Behrens and the AEG, 1907–1914*, trans.
Iain Boyd Whyte, The MIT Press, Cambridge, Mass., 1984.
28 Quoted on p. 177.
29 It thereby brought to life, with uniquely German features, the sort of reformed
work environment envisaged a generation earlier by William Morris and the
founders of the Arts and Crafts Guilds in England. See Frederic J. Schwartz, *The
Werkbund: Design Theory and Mass Culture before the First World War*, op. cit.,
pp. 58–59.

people. This sort of production was, of course, a major reason for the rapid spread of German products into other markets throughout Europe.

Behrens's work for AEG also demonstrated the vital inter-dependence of product design and building design. It reinforced the idea, firmly held by many of the organisers of the Werkbund, that altering public sensibilities by introducing changes in the design of objects would encourage new ways of thinking about architecture. In 1902, for example, Muthesius asserted that once the arts and crafts had laid the groundwork foran artistic culture, architecture would assume "leadershipin the community of arts".[30] Admitting that this eventualitywas still some time off, he could only ask, "When will our architecture be ready to assume this responsibility?"[31] The astounding success of German artistic production in the succeeding decade seemed to make this transfer of artistic control imminent.

By 1911, however, Muthesius was becoming impatient. Even if he was rightfully proud of German accomplishments in product design and the modernisation of building interiors, architecture still lagged:

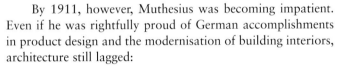

Peter Behrens, design for a brochure for a table fan, 1912. Behrens designed the fan in 1908

> The fortunate progress of the arts and crafts movement, which has given new shape to the interior decoration of our rooms, breathed fresh life into handicrafts and imparted fruitful inspiration to architecture, may be regarded as only a minor prelude to what must come. For in spite of all we have achieved we are still wading up to our knees in the brutalisation of forms. If proof is needed we have only to observe the fact that our country is being covered daily and hourly with buildings of the most inferior character, unworthy of our age and calculated to speak to posterity all too eloquently of our epoch's lack of culture. … If a nation produces good furniture and good light fittings, but daily erects the worst possible buildings, this can only be a sign of

30 Muthesius, *Style-Architecture and Building-Art*, op. cit., p. 99.
31 Ibid.

heterogeneous, unclarified conditions, conditions whose very inconsistency is proof of the lack of discipline and organisation.[32]

Bruno Taut, pavilion for the steel industry at the building exhibition, Leipzig, 1913

In a speech to the Werkbund that same year, Muthesius echoed a widely held sentiment that Germany was capable of far more than it had achieved so far: "Germany enjoys a reputation for the most strict and exact organisation in her businesses, heavy industry and state institutions of any country in the world – our military discipline may be cited as the ground of this. Such being the case, perhaps this is an expression of Germany's vocation – to resolve the great problem of architectonic form."[33] The solution to this problem proved to be elusive. With the exception of a few essentially unrelated buildings – factories designed by Behrens, exhibition pavilions by Bruno Taut, houses by Heinrich Tessenow, Hermann Muthesius and Richard Riemerschmid – architecture was slow to manifest the changes that had so profoundly affected the design of domestic interiors and furnishings.

As a witness to these conditions, Jeanneret was similarly aware of the great successes, but also of the vulnerability of Germany in the domain of artistic production. So it was not with false optimism that he concluded his report with bets on

32 Hermann Muthesius, "Aims of the Werkbund", in *Programs and Manifestoes on 20th-Century Architecture*, ed. Ulrich Conrads, The MIT Press, Cambridge, Mass., 1970, pp. 26–27.
33 Muthesius, "Wo stehen wir?" quoted in Reyner Banham, *Theory and Design in the First Machine Age*, 2nd edn, The MIT Press, Cambridge, Massachusetts, 1960, p. 76 (original page not cited). The things in which Germans put such faith during the years before the First World War – business, heavy industry, military discipline – became sources of great disillusionment after the war. It was already clear to some at the time that the lack of a German style in the early years of the twentieth century had been partly the consequence of the overproduction of commodities by business and heavy industry. See Georg Simmel, "The Metropolis and Mental Life" [1903], in *The Sociology of Georg Simmel*, ed. H. Wolf, Free Press, New York, 1950, p. 410. See also Schwartz, op. cit., p. 29, and Francesco Dal Co, *Figures of Architecture and Thought: German Architecture Culture 1880–1920*, Rizzoli, New York, 1990, p. 60.

116

Raymond Duchamp-Villon, entrance to the Salon
Bourgeois at the Salon d'Automne, Paris, 1912

Charles-Édouard Jeanneret, interior of the Villa Jeanneret, c. 1912. Jeanneret chose bold patterns and an eclectic mix of traditional furniture, similar to the French designers associated with the Salon Bourgeois in Paris

Le Corbusier, interior perspective for *Immeuble-Villas,* 1922. The drawing shows early versions of the *casiers standard* and other furniture reminiscent of German designs from a decade earlier

France, saying, "Germany, for the last one or two years especially, is returning again to follow the footsteps of the giants of the arts of France." And holding out hope for the French decorative arts, he asked, "Will a France suffocated by Germany escape from its lethargy in the area of applied art? Precursory signs have appeared at the last two 'Salons d'Automne'."[34]

Although it would not be quite proper to hold out Jeanneret's own rise to prominence in Paris after the war as confirmation of his predictions of 1912, he no doubt perceived his role in the development of modern architecture as an outcome, partially, of his experience with the decorative arts movement in Germany. In 1925, Le Corbusier answered Muthesius's question of two decades before, announcing in *The Decorative Art of Today* that architecture had finally assumed "leadership in the community of arts" – that "the hour of architecture" had come to fruition. "Decorative art," he said, "has raised from its cradle the new consciousness born of the machine …"[35] But this time it was in France that this momentous change had come about. Le Corbusier argued that, while Germany had benefited from England and France before the war, it was France, bolstered by an understanding of German accomplishments and spurred by competition with Germany, that achieved the final synthesis of modern architecture. He explained the succession this way:

---

34 Quoted on p. 204. Although clearly not yet a threat to German production, French designers such as André Mare and his collaborators in the *Maison Cubiste* exhibition of 1912 were beginning to develop new directions for the decorative arts that promised to challenge German dominance in the field. For an account of Jeanneret's relationships with the progressive French interior designers before the First World War, see Nancy J. Troy, *Modernism and the Decorative Arts in France – Art Nouveau to Le Corbusier,* Yale University Press, New Haven and London, 1991, pp. 103–58.
35 Le Corbusier, *The Decorative Art of Today,* op. cit., p. 132.

The sweet voice of Ruskin – "Look, here are the flowers, the insects, and the beasts of the Good Lord." Soul of Giotto. Delight in primitives. *Pre-Raphaelitism*. Here in rational France the appeal to nature; analysis. The entomologist Fabre excited us. We realised that natural phenomena have an organisation, and we *opened our eyes*. 1900. An outpouring. Truly a fine moment!

Then Germany, working twenty-four hours a day, seized the moment. Her painters built houses – Darmstadt and after. But houses have no life without structure. All that great noise was for nothing. Nothing came out of it all. Still, there was a stimulus.

The Munich people came to Paris in 1912 *[sic]*. The Salon d'Automne. The *ensembliers*. … Cubism, so profoundly serious in the hands of its authors, is evidence that everything was called into question. Around 1910 it already showed the pressures for revolt and the ascetic virility appropriate to conspirators bent on overturning the established order. This was achieved. …

A new conception has been born. Decoration is no longer possible. Our effusions, our vivid awareness of the beauties and power of nature have found their place in the framework of architecture.[36]

Jeanneret's intimate knowledge of the decorative arts movement in Germany, and his affinity with the circle of Cubists involved with the decorative arts in France, prepared him well for the extraordinarily influential architectural work he undertook in Paris during the early 1920s. Clearly, his own development, and the development of the architectural movement into which he inserted himself, was strongly affected by German design before the First World War. Jeanneret's *Study of the Decorative Art Movement in Germany* is thus, in many ways, an important text for the history of modern architecture. It presents not only a clear assessment of the decorative arts at their height in Germany, but it also helps to describe the competitive environment in France that spurred the development of modern architecture, a movement in which Le Corbusier played a crucial role.

36 Ibid., p. 137.

Carl Eduard Biermann, *Borsigs Maschinenbauanstalt zu Berlin*, 1847.
Oil on canvas, 105.5 x 156.5 cm, Stadtmuseum Berlin

I

Charles-Édouard Jeanneret (Le Corbusier), watch case made of
gold, silver, copper, steel and diamonds, 1906. FLC

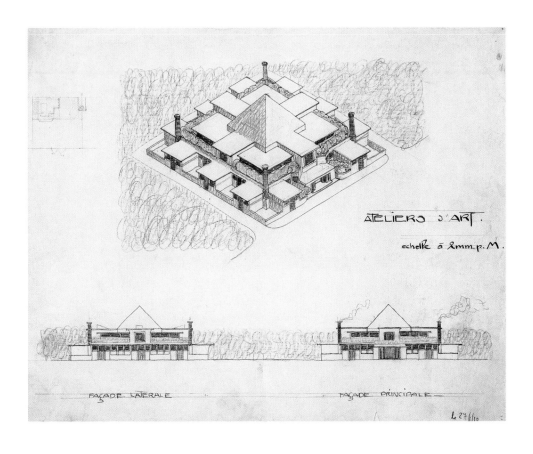

ATELIERS D'ART.

echelle à 2mm.p.M.

FAÇADE LATÉRALE

FAÇADE PRINCIPALE

L 27/6/10

Charles-Édouard Jeanneret, design for the *Ateliers d'Arts* building in
La Chaux-de-Fonds, January 1911.
Pencil and coloured pencil on paper, 31 x 40 cm, Centre Georges Pompidou

III

Charles-Édouard Jeanneret, diary sketch of the interior design
for the art dealers Brakl, Munich, 1910

IV

Emmanuel von Seidl, interior design for the art dealers Brakl, Munich, 1910

Ernst Ludwig Kirchner, *Sich kämmender Akt*, 1913.
Oil on canvas, 125 x 90 cm, Brücke-Museum Berlin

Charles-Édouard Jeanneret, *Vin d'Athos*, 1913.
Pencil and watercolour on paper, 42.4 x 45 cm, FLC

VII

Heinrich Tessenow, Festival Hall design for Hellerau garden city, 1910–12.
Entrance facade

Charles-Édouard Jeanneret, Villa Schwob, 1916

Lucian Bernhard, Advertisement for Manoli, 1910. Colour lithograph, 69.5 x 95 cm

Charles-Édouard Jeanneret, *Le bol rouge*, 1919. Oil on canvas, 81 x 65 cm, FLC

Charles-Édouard Jeanneret, bureau for his mother, c. 1915/16, FLC

Le Corbusier, *casier standard*, 1925. Nationalmuseum Stockholm

Le Corbusier, cover of *L'Art décoratif d'aujourd'hui*, 1925

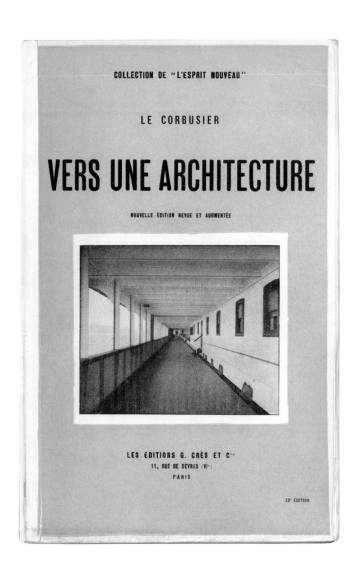

Le Corbusier, cover of *Vers une architecture*, 1923

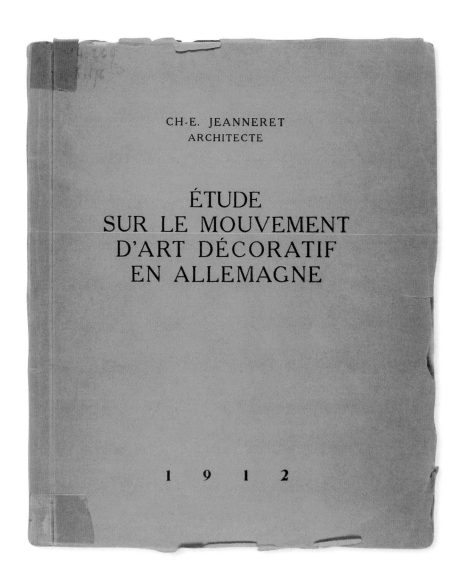

CH-E. JEANNERET
ARCHITECTE

ÉTUDE
SUR LE MOUVEMENT
D'ART DÉCORATIF
EN ALLEMAGNE

1 9 1 2

Charles-Édouard Jeanneret, cover of
Étude sur le mouvement d'art décoratif en Allemagne, 1912

XVI

Charles-Édouard Jeanneret
(Le Corbusier)

A STUDY
OF THE DECORATIVE
ART MOVEMENT
IN GERMANY

1912

The Commission of the École d'Art, in its meeting of 22 February 1912, resolved to publish the report on the Decorative Art Movement in Germany presented to it by Mr Ch.-Éd. Jeanneret, convinced that the information it contains must be publicised in the interest of developing the Decorative Arts in our country.

The Secretary   *The President*
G. MOSER   H. BOPP-BOILLOT

I had been living in Munich for two months when I received a letter drawn up by Mr L'Eplattenier in the name of the Commission of the École d'Art whose business-like tone clearly indicated the direction of study that I was being asked to undertake; here are some characteristic passages:

"Believing that you could study with great profit for us the considerable progress being made by the applied arts in Germany, the Commission of the École d'Art has resolved to entrust you with this task, if you agree to it, and contingent upon a subsidy that will be requested from the authorities. You would provide a report on everything that concerns professional training, the organisation of the art trades, the creation, fabrication and sale of artistic productions; you could include notes on all that concerns art in the city and in architecture – in brief, on all that might promote the development of art and beauty here in our country."

This proposition appealed to me very much; I accepted and expressed my gratitude to the Commission for the confidence it was prepared to place in me. It so happens that the purpose of my stay in Germany had been to study the production of art, and the Commission thus gave me the opportunity to open doors that might otherwise have remained closed to an inquisitor without official credentials. I had a feel for this study and had already established solid connections that would inevitably lead me to others. In 1908 I had been offered employment in Vienna, upon presentation of my drawings, by Josef Hoffmann of the Wiener Werkstätte; this connection was to be of constant use to me in Germany. Upon my arrival in Munich I made the acquaintance

141

of Prof. Theodor Fischer; our relations were, thanks to his great kindness, more friendly than businesslike; and likewise with Baron Günther von Pechmann, director of the "Vermittlungsstelle für angewandte Kunst". Then, at the time of my first journey to Berlin, [I met] Prof. Peter Behrens (in whose office I subsequently worked as a designer for five months); [and] Dr Hermann Muthesius. During my trips to Dresden, it was Mr Wolf Dohrn, acting director of the Werkbund; Heinrich Tessenow, architect of the town of Hellerau. Finally, on my travels, Mr Osthaus, in Hagen, the director of the "Museum Folkwang" and of the "Deutsches Museum".

I am indebted to these Men – upon whom one must confer the epithet "gentlemen" – to these affable men, to these courageous men, for most of the knowledge that I was fortunate enough to acquire. Official recommendations were supplied by Mr Alfred de Claparède, Swiss Minister in Berlin, on the request made to him in writing by Mr Robert Comtesse. Mr de Claparède is ensured of my deepest gratitude for the attention he was so kind to devote to this matter.

The letter of the Commission alluded, through the various passages that I have noted, to such vast terrain that I must refrain at this point from responding thoroughly to all of it. In spite of the limits within which I have determined to remain, I see this report already becoming excessively voluminous and thus exceeding, on account of the fatigue it will cause the reader, the limits of usefulness. I have, of course, opened my eyes during the course of these thirty months, but I will not report anything but that which constitutes the direct and practical interests of this study: research, down to its very heart, into the vital line of this organism of **applied art** in Germany, an organism so quickly arrived at maturity, whose strength, whose life, we find to be incredibly powerful.

I

GENERAL CONSIDERATIONS

GENERAL CONSIDERATIONS

THE REVIVAL

HERE is what today's innovators claim:

Until the Revolution, the Arts, faithful expression of the economic and political life and of the psychological state of the people, arose slowly and without faltering, through evolution, out of the obscure Middle Ages to the utmost refinement and delicacy. Born of the people and for the people, they became, little by little, the monopoly of the cultured and wealthy classes.

Then, the Revolution overthrows everything. Men who have received an indifferent education, who have arisen from the ignorant masses, attain power – or have the prospect of attaining it. Until then, their new responsibilities had been fulfilled by noblemen. In the domain of Art, especially, this succession must have been hopeless. But, forced to accept it nevertheless, these men inevitably committed **improprieties**, improprieties that were bound to be disastrous for Art.

However, the thousands of artisans had not yet disappeared; they had been the astounding craftsmen (architects, carpenters, sculptors, stucco-workers, iron-workers) of the most delicate styles that had ever existed in Europe. Their practised hands and eyes were destined to recover their crafts from past troubles. And so it was in France, where the Phrygian cap had been deified, that with absolute poetry the resurrection of ancient times was mobilised. So strong was the tradition of art that neither the hand nor the eye could betray it, and the "Empire Style" was created, the style that remains perhaps the most aristocratic, the most sober, the most "serious". This, say today's innovators, is the style that is surely the closest to us. They say further: "It is, logically, the style that we must take up and carry on." The sons of the artisans of the Empire still knew how to work, even if the great inspiration dissipated and passed on with the Emperor, ceding place to an increasingly obtrusive bourgeois vitality. They acquired enough of this admirable tradition to leave for us the Restoration (in Germany the "Biedermeier" – from the sobriquet given to a level-headed country gentleman, a little too anxious to appear to good advantage, but yet full of honesty). The style is charming; it brings us the ethereal impression of crinolines and of cashmere shawls slipping from demure shoulders, and of pretty faces framed by tresses in vertical registers, buried under impressive hats of pliant straw hanging with ribbons. The effect was total: bourgeoisism triumphed everywhere, in politics as in private life; this was the Second Empire, and then the great disorder, "the post-War years".

They claim therefore, the moderns of today, to perpetuate "the Empire" after having mastered the more facile "Biedermeier". **They want to renew the thread of tradition.** They say: artisans, subjugated by the tastes of the masses, are dead; yes, the applied Arts, suffocated by external circumstances, fell into the most lamentable state; they remained so while the fine arts inherited the libertarian breath of the Revolution and entered into a new era. In effect, the applied Arts uttered their last words in the anaemic forms of the Louis-Philippe – while Delacroix roared with Rude, and Courbet showed his mettle by pulling down the tyrannical column, after having painted his defiant canvases; he personified the Genius of those who were to come. Manet had classical blood in his veins, and a pioneer's soul stirred him; under public derision, he incised with an indelible stroke the way to health. Renoir, Monet, Sisley, Pissarro followed his trail, while Cézanne strode as one destined to open immense horizons. Some of these geniuses expressed their creed almost sick at heart (because of the jeers of the crowd that rendered them fearful). Van Gogh died a madman; Gauguin fled Europe to find calm on a forgotten island among peaceable savages.

And from all of this was born an alphabet of colour unknown until then, with avenging power and unimaginable delicacy. And reason, joined with love of beauty, proclaimed definitively the separation of "painting" from "sculpture". This was no doubt the greatest **"Reconquest"**. Since then each is asserting itself, naked and disconcerting for the crowd still attached to its lazy ways – sculpture enamoured of form, painting mad about colours; already Rhythm enters in and declares: Order is imposing itself; let us see that it succeeds. They believe, these moderns, that today is one of the most beautiful epochs and that twenty years will give rise to painting and sculpture just as beautiful, just as productive, as are these times. It appears as if history will not contradict them.

And yet they call themselves the "classicists". The word becomes absurd in their mouths – or prophetic. They followed the path of tradition, the persistent elevation of the race. They watched madmen, degenerates, then blind men grasp the brush, the acerbic word, to render the pitiless verdict and, lifted to the Institute on the respected altars of the crowd, to be contemptuous of **"fine painting"**, of **"fine sculpture"**, contemptuous of colour, contemptuous of form. They have watched these men

146

monopolise opinion and persecute those who do not think like them. And so they found themselves in the shadows again, subject to the laugh of the bourgeois crowd and the sneers of the academics. They felt the urge; they felt themselves numerous; they became conscious of their sincerity. And to the scornful attacks of the complacent, they counterattacked; war was declared …

The battleground is once again Paris …

They will be, in their turn, unmerciful; they are young, a little foolish, they exaggerate. They laugh. To the works that they say were born in the caves and of the dust of the underworld, under melancholy skulls, they contrast foolish gaiety, exuberant life … And one absolutely must not, when one sees such exuberance, such excesses, one must not lift one's head and say: "They are fools!" but one must remember that their masters were bruised old men, humble – the most humble – conscientious – the most conscientious – honest – the most honest! – Delacroix, Courbet, Manet, Daumier, Cézanne, Van Gogh …

And parallel with the fine arts, literature undertook the same struggles, won the same victories. And music places César Franck like a tower on a ridge finally scaled from which one sees new territory.

Meanwhile the applied arts were ceasing to live, despite Grasset, despite Ruskin, despite Morris …

. . . .

During this time unformed Germany struggled along and achieved nothing; she copied France, for centuries … until the War. She was more suited than anyone to accept bourgeoisism: she nurtured it into its most definitive expressions; since she did not have a tradition and her disorganisation paralysed her true inventive spirit. (I do not speak here, of course, of the popular folk arts which are no more German than Bulgarian, than Swedish, than Hungarian; the popular arts are above all **human**, thus international.) In effect, Germany, after having exhausted French Gothic, expressed nothing more, after the Renaissance (which was reasonably self-possessed as had been the State at that time), then the Baroque from Italy, then the Louis XIV, XV, XVI from France, then the Empire from Paris and finally the Restoration from Paris again. Her peasant art, on the other hand, remained her more normal and her more beautiful expression, proving to be, until then, a great calm among the immovable masses of the people. But then 1870. **Germany Triumphs!**

Concentration, unification. She becomes a single body. It is total victory, and her people are robust and youthful at heart.

Pride showed on their faces; the bourgeois became arrogant; and so they intensified their state! and this was without question an extraordinary moment in the arts of European peoples. They were its witnesses, the cities that were born then: Berlin suddenly outspread, Munich renewed, the Stuttgart of post-1870! Economic prosperity was born; cities springing up, swollen with factories, with squalid streets, with palaces out of nothingness, immense, and of inexcusable taste; a voyage across Germany instructs at length on this subject. However, the seat of this mood and of this expansion certainly seems to have been Berlin, with its emperor who lives in the midst of the satellites that he has gathered around himself. And this mood inscribes in immense letters on every stone pride, triumph, an affront to the vanquished (and to taste): The Palace of the Reichstag, the Dome, the monument to Wilhelm I in front of the palace, and the column of victory, symbolic of power – of that ugliness also ... that becomes beautiful by force of character!

It is clear that in this state of mind Germany remained outside the idealistic preoccupations of the rebellious painters of Paris. She created her State, her industry, her commerce, her army; she gave nothing to painting but a Feuerbach incarnating one side of her sentimental and romantic soul, while Böcklin incarnated the other, but a Schwind dreaming of sheepfolds in the mountains or in the villages of the provinces, but a Menzel who came, like a happy coincidence, to paint the people with a very resolute brush. And yet Germany also produced a Hans von Marées whose genius must have been intolerable to his own country and who went off to commune with himself in Pompeii; a Leibl, whom friendship and special affinity tied to Courbet. The galleries filled with enormous battle scenes or with the French fleeing before pointed helmets. Now here is an aspect of something new and unexpected: France persists in renouncing its painters and sculptors, the Institute condemns and undermines them. But Germany positions itself as a champion of modernism, creating nothing in the fine arts to prove itself so, but revealing its new tastes through the systematic absorption (purchase) of the works of Parisian painters and sculptors (Courbet, Manet, Cézanne, van Gogh, Matisse, Maillol, etc.) and, on the other hand, revealing itself almost without warning to be colossal in power, in determination and in achievement in the applied arts. These facts clearly place the two countries face to face; revolutionised Germany, evolved France. This is an accidental occurrence in Germany, which today is steering towards a disproportion between inadequate roots and excessive flower. This is because of a sudden victory, an instantaneous blooming; it is an event of passing order. France is making a slow effort of concentration having to fight against what one could call "the laziness of the family son". There is economic revolution in Germany, because of the war and artistic dictatorship by some strong, rational minds. There is in France normal, progressive evolution of thought, of the soul of her people.

I detail the case of Germany: she was victorious by surprise in 1870; she was stupefied by it, then enchanted, then proud, arrogant. She organised herself, spread out, bloomed, swelled, objectively affirmed herself as a considerable new force; she proved it with her construction of fantastic warships, of barracks, of formidable arsenals, then of gigantic, disproportionate, immoderate palaces. Into the domain of art, of this swelling up of building, there came architects, brusquely torn from their tranquil bourgeoisism, and with them horrible works; from there came architects of the following generation who had that nation's rational spirit and its triumphant ardour and who profited from the lessons of their predecessors; and there were thus works astonishing for their youthfulness, then for rationality, then for suitability, and the obstacle of routines was surmounted, and, as the roots did not cut deeply enough into the humus of the nation, satisfaction for successful work arrived and with it the arrogance that swells itself up once again.

It was an economic, thus **practical**, revolution. Opportunistic artists, whom the circumstances suddenly made great, like a Murat, like a Hoche, like a Ney, gravitated at once into a practical sphere. Political, commercial and industrial expansion gave them cause to resolve the problems of utility and high modernism: public building, schools and administrations, factories with workers' estates, train stations, markets, slaughterhouses, auditoriums, theatres, music halls, garden cities. Of a positive temperament in this positive hour, they fully resolved the problems that were put to them; they made themselves strong, practical and very active; they exploited the most effective propaganda; they created: exhibitions of all sorts; art journals, which they transformed into radically new organisms with profound repercussions for the masses; conferences and then competitions; and they arrived upon their miraculous success – arising from an economic and political revolution – face to face with the great social problems which they claim to resolve through art, through harmony.

Intoxicated with success, they have an unlimited faith, which produces results.

Throughout this prodigious evolution, they reflected an enthusiasm, a vitality, a discipline above all, an admirable practical sense and inspired opportunism; they demolished the ivory towers that, in France, increasingly separate the artists from the crowd; they made themselves populist, socialist, imperialist, as the occasions demanded, with the speed of cunning speculators. The administrative fortresses were simultaneously overthrown and cleared away; the princely courts were conquered, and their princes wanting to take the lead – and like Maecenas of old buying self-respect – they disbursed wealth and encouraged initiatives. They work in support of their emperor, the man with the pointed helmet, the man of the Dome, of the Reich-stag, of the monument to Kaiser-Wilhelm I, of the Siegessäule. They will clothe him ultimately in the toga of Pericles ... Pericles at the helm of a dreadnought!

What distinguished the new orientation in the "applied" arts in Germany from the outset, was, along with the Ruskinian reform, the accidental revelation of the arts of Japan. The ground was no doubt favourable, because the assimilation was radical. The echoes of the Ruskinian crusade immured France, Belgium, England. France did not know how to understand nor to sustain the effort of a Grasset. Belgium gave her-self over to exaggerations (van de Velde); England found almost nothing new to say, so much did their art of building houses remain adequate to their customs. Vienna offered a receptive terrain and revolutionised itself by Japanising. A superior mental-ity, like that of Otto Wagner, revealed itself there. His two students Olbrich and Hoff-mann will play a major role. Josef Hoffmann imposes his irresistible personality and becomes the soul of an unparalleled speculative enterprise – the "Wiener Werkstätte" – that is casting a brilliance, as yet unmatched, on Vienna.

Olbrich, after having built the Vienna Secession, is called to Darmstadt by the Grand Duke of Hesse. There he becomes the centre of a colony of artists–artisans; he overwhelms Germany with his Secessionist works, while superior minds, bound to tradition by their temperaments and their studies, make a favourable counterpoint to his extravagances (Theodor Fischer – Munich, Messel – Berlin). Men devoted to matters of art abandon the brush and concentrate their efforts on architecture: Peter Behrens, the painter from Munich and Darmstadt, becomes the director of the department of architecture in Düsseldorf, then advisor to AEG, the colossal electricity enterprise in Berlin. Bruno Paul, caricaturist for Simplicissimus, is appointed director of the school of Berlin (architecture and decorative art); Bernhard Pankok, painter, is director of the school in Stuttgart (interior architecture and decorative art). Wilhelm Debschitz, painter, creates a new school of decorative art and interior architecture.

Many countries within one great country, Prussia, Bavaria, Württemberg, Saxony, etc., divide the movement and deprive it of the unified character that it has assumed in Vienna. It is more dull, more fragmented; there is the school of Berlin, of Dresden, of Munich, of Stuttgart, all fundamentally different.

Among the great powers, Germany plays an essentially active role in the realm of applied arts. One need only remember her eloquent manifestations at the exhibitions of Turin 1902, St Louis 1904, Milan 1906, Brussels 1910 and finally the Paris Salon d'Automne in 1910. France contributed nothing in these same events. This year, I saw her shamefully represented in Rome, and it seems as if she wants to show that she likes to make a fool of herself. What are the factors that give Germany her strength? What are the workings of this astounding organism? This is what was interesting to know. It is what I was asked to find out; it is what I will strive to report as faithfully as possible. What I saw in those twelve months of 1910–1911 is so complex that I will have great difficulty being succinct, and even more, being clear and therefore useful.

II

GERMAN INITIATIVES AND PRODUCTIONS

GERMAN INITIATIVES AND PRODUCTIONS

COLLECTIVE EFFORTS
ORGANISATION – PROPAGANDA

The "Werkbund", the "Deutsches Museum für Kunst im Handel und Gewerbe". "Vermittlungsstelle für angewandte Kunst". "Ausstellung München", etc.

Artists and tradesmen want to lend each other mutual support. This partnership and this undisputed purpose are the soul of all the enterprises of which I will speak.

THE WERKBUND
(The Alliance for Production)

THE "Alliance for Production" was founded in 1908 with "the goal of uniting artists, manufacturers and industrial enterprises so as to ennoble, through an effective collaboration, the senses of taste and technique in German production," and this "by means of education and propaganda."

"The members of the Society may be artists, artisans (private individuals or commercial and industrial firms) or any men competent in the commercial and artistic domains."

"The Alliance for Production" is constituted as follows:
The Management; the Board; the Assembly of members in an annual congress.

On my way to Berlin, I had the opportunity to travel with Baron Günther von Pechmann, director of the "Vermittlungsstelle für Angewandte Kunst" in Munich. I was going to the "Städtebau-Ausstellung" (town planning exhibition); it so happened that he was on his way to the "Werkbund" Congress. He was kind enough to invite me there, and for three days I followed all the peregrinations of the

Congress participants throughout Berlin. What I saw during those three days impressed me, and I wanted to acquaint myself with this powerful instrument of the "Werkbund".

My research was facilitated by a fortunate encounter with Mr Wolf Dohrn, the acting director of the "Werkbund", with whom I formed personal ties. It is to him that I am indebted for most of the information that will constitute the most characteristic part of my report.

According to its founders, The "Werkbund" must be a consecration of previous efforts, and must lend them, along with the certainty of success, a general, national significance.

The efforts so far realised are such that the "Werkbund" will play a major role in the area of German culture. Here are the facts:

On the 5th and 6th of October 1907, "The Alliance for Production" was founded in Munich. Following a discourse on German industry, on its productions and on its situation in the culture of our time, a number of artists and artisans, as well as a certain number of friends of the arts, at the invitation of a preliminary corporation of twelve artists and twelve firms, resolved to found the "Alliance for Production".

... At the end of 1908 (one year later), the society included 600 members; at the end of 1909, more than 800.

The Society is a union of tradesmen. **The admission of members is not made at the request of interested parties, nor by referral, but solely on an invitation from the board of the Society.**

In this way, **the Society demonstrates its determination to marshal capable forces in the arts, in industry, in the trades and in commerce. It wants to encourage collaboration among all of the capabilities that presently exist in the arts and craft disciplines;** whether this involves purely active, practical and commercial forces with progressive inclinations, or idealistic forces.

It forms the rallying point for all those who are talented and capable, for all those who consider the domain of applied arts to be a part (and not the lesser) of cultural work, who want to ensure, for themselves and for others, a centre that represents their interests in the purposeful development of their progressive ideas.

The goal of the Society is therefore "the ennobling of the crafts through the collaboration of art, industry and commerce, by means of education and propaganda." Thus the Society acts as representative for tradesmen in everything that concerns artistic improvement. Furthermore, it will take an interest in anything that might contribute to the improvement of industrial production.

In order to accomplish its mission in these areas, the society recruits members from the front lines of groups participating in artistic research. It therefore searches first of all among the manufacturing industries, particularly in the domain of the decorative arts.

The selection of members, then, is one of its most important undertakings; I provide some names here, which will make anyone who knows a little about modern Germany mindful of what such a union might achieve in hands like these:

The directing members are: Royal Councillor Peter Bruckmann, "in Firma Peter Bruckmann und Söhne", Heilbronn (first President); Prof. Dr Theodor Fischer, architect, Munich (second President); Gustav Gericke, director of the linoleum factory Delmenhorst; Painter Gustav Klimt, Vienna; Privy Councillor Dr Engineer Hermann Muthesius, Berlin; Prof. J. Scharvogel, director of the ceramics manufacturer, Darmstadt; Dr Wolf Dohrn, Dresden, acting director of the "Werkbund".

Each city or principality has a "trusted representative" to speak for regional interests. Among other well-known names: Berlin, Prof. Bruno Möhring; Austria, Vienna, Josef Hoffmann; Bavaria, Munich, Prof. Richard Riemerschmid; Thuringia, Weimar, Prof. Henry van de Velde; Westphalia, Hagen, Karl-Ernst Osthaus, etc. Other selected members: Peter Behrens, architect, Berlin; Eugen Diederichs, publisher, Jena; Karl Klingspor, "in Firma Klingspor" (type foundry); Prof. Wilhelm Kreis, Düsseldorf; Bernhard Pankok, Stuttgart; Prof. Bruno Paul, Berlin; Dr Karl Schmidt "in Firma Deutsche Werkstätte für Handwerkskunst GmbH", Dresden.

In addition, each craft has a representative for its particular interests: construction (including that of gardens); the ceramics industry; glassmaking; furniture and interior architecture; metalworking, etc. The activity of the Society consists of propagandist and avant-garde initiatives. This was the case, for example, at the following exhibitions:

a) **"Exhibition for an Architectural Improvement of the Construction of Factories"**, in the form of a unified collection designed as a travelling exhibition; the purpose of the exhibition is, first of all, to advise industry of the architectural possibilities that exist for the construction of factories. It is currently making its way through the industrial districts of Germany and Austria.

b) Participation of the members of the "Werkbund" in the "Exhibition for Christian Art" in Düsseldorf 1909. Special exhibition of the "Werkbund" in Brussels 1910. Collaboration of the Society in the "II. Ton-, Zement-, Kalkindustrie-Ausstellung" in Berlin 1910 ("Exhibition of the Clay, Cement and Lime Industries", details below). Following these exhibitions, the "Werkbund" resolved to direct its efforts most particularly toward the area of **the exhibition**; thus it is that the "Werkbund", in collaboration with the "Deutsches Museum" (which will be discussed below), is organising an exhibition intended for all fields of art and decorative art to be held in the Spring of 1912 at the "Zoologischer Garten" in Berlin, on **the quality of presentation**.

For an **"Exhibition of the Printing and Graphics Industries"** in Frankfurt 1912, the "Werkbund", along with the "Deutsches Museum" of Hagen, will host groups involved with book printing and graphic art.

In addition, the "Werkbund" has announced its probable collaboration in the **"Exhibition for the Arts of Building"** in Leipzig 1913.

One of the principal creations of the "Werkbund" was the "German Museum for Art in Commerce and Industry". Actually, the idea came from the "Folkwang" museum in Hagen, whose director and proprietor, Karl-Ernst Osthaus, proposed it at one of the congressional assemblies of the "Werkbund" (details of this institution will be discussed below).

In addition to exhibitions, the "Werkbund" is undertaking an active propaganda effort by means of publications whose uncomplicated titles describe their sympathies from the outset:

"Gewerbliche Materialkunde" (Science of Industrial Materials) published under the auspices of the "Alliance for Production" by Dr Paul Krais, Tübingen.

A guide through artistic Berlin edited by the "Werkbund" permitting one to discover easily ancient and modern works of art, buildings, monuments, **institutes, firms, shops, apartment buildings** which, above all, can interest the visitor fond of Art and curious about its present state of evolution.

A whole series of annual brochures published in the form of reports in which are announced promising creations or innovations fulfilling goals analogous to those of the society.

Propaganda by means of lectures is certainly one of the most effective arms of the "Alliance for Production".

There were, for example, courses on the "Ornamentation of the Surface" (Flächenverzierung), given by outstanding members of the Society, aimed at the artistic development of designers in the factories, particularly those in the textile industry.

Then lectures on the **"Artistic Education of the German Merchant"** on the request of the "Deutscher Verband für das Kaufmännische Unterrichtswesen" (German Society for the Education of the Merchant) with the collaboration of the Chamber of Commerce and Industry. The first series took place in the jurisdiction of the Chambers of Commerce of Saxony and Hanover, the second in Berlin, the third in the coastal cities of the North. The lectures were concluded with a small exhibition in the "Museum for Art in Commerce and Industry". The Exhibition was entitled "Art in the Service of the Merchant".

After six lectures on the education of taste in the merchant, two others were given on the **"Arrangement of the Interior in the Home"**; one on **"The Question of Truth or the Question of Appearance"**; one on **"Fashion and Taste"**; one on the **"Decoration of Shop Fronts"**; about 5000 salesmen and saleswomen took part in these lectures. For 1911, a cycle relating to the Saxon textile industry and also to the textile industry of the Rhine was anticipated.

For the organisation of these courses and lectures, the "Werkbund" sent out a call to speakers and conference organisers, requesting a list of their topics so that it could respond with the most judicious choice to numerous requests that had already been addressed to it by chambers of commerce and by industry. In this area, the "Werkbund" has fixed its condition thus: 100 marks as honorarium will be guaranteed to the speaker for each lecture, and his first-class travel expenses will be covered.

In order to furnish outstanding documentation to all authors, speakers or professors, the "Werkbund" , in cooperation with the "Deutsches Museum" of Hagen, has founded a **Centre for Transparencies** and a **Centre for Illustrations**. The latter, having been founded specifically to promote the German exhibition in Brussels, has been closed, its task being considered finished.

Finally, the "Werkbund" has just established the "College of Art and Decoration" (concerning arrangement of shops and shop fronts) in Berlin, so as to promote and to highlight the tremendous gains that have appeared in the area of the Retail Showroom. This school takes ten pupils each month. The course lasts two months. From the beginning, the school displayed tremendous activity, especially around the great competition for shop fronts in Berlin, where it obtained the highest award.

Announcing these results in its report, the "Werkbund" advised its "trusted representatives" from various cities and provinces to organise similar competitions. Since, it declares, this is the best means of entering into communication with the merchants of the locality.

Noting this, the "Union for the Education of Merchants" has decided to support the education of young merchants in collaboration with the "Deutsches Museum" of Hagen.

Apart from realising goals the "Werkbund" sets for itself, the organisation continues to expand, particularly in the augmentation of relations with Austria. Steps are also being made for the inclusion of Holland in the society of the "Alliance for Production".

And, just so that no one ignores it – [particularly] those with a vital, working interest in the initiatives of the "Werkbund" – the society sends its report each year to the imperial authorities, to those of the states of the Empire, as well as to representatives of Commerce and Industry (Chambers of Commerce and Industry), and likewise to the chairs of corporations.

In this way, then, all of Germany feels united against ugliness and united in the goal of bringing about **beautiful industry**. It is as if **everyone** is working for the "Werkbund"; the "Werkbund" is invigorating everyone. Each is striving in his sphere – Commerce, Industry, Art – and what results is a fruitful solidarity. As in a triptych, each panel is conceived to be beautiful, but for the beauty of the ensemble.

DEUTSCHES MUSEUM
FÜR KUNST IM HANDEL UND GEWERBE
HAGEN I.W.
(German museum for Art in Trade and Industry.)

This is a travelling museum.

It was proposed, as I have said, by the well-known patron, Mr Ernst Osthaus, in Hagen, and accepted unanimously by the participants in the annual "Werkbund" Congress at Frankfurt, in 1909.

They felt that various efforts in the decorative arts were too oblivious of one another. An architect might clearly recall having seen certain choice materials, fabrics, or tiles – a businessman certain posters or prospectuses – a merchant certain ceramics, jewellery, etc., but either he would be unable to find out, or could not remember, where they came from. It was essential, therefore, to develop some sort of mechanism for publicity, for education and for information, "**to allow the image of our age to assert itself even more strongly**".

In order to shake off the apathy of a certain few, to encourage the hopes of some, and to bring about resolutions, it was essential to bring together all of the accomplishments originating in noteworthy groups whose efforts circumstances had favoured.

The city of Hagen, in Westphalia, was chosen to be the seat of this new museum because of the spark that had already been ignited there – its "Museum Folkwang" (this is the museum containing one of the most complete collections of Parisian painters and sculptors, of which I spoke at the beginning of this report) – and also because of its geographical and industrial situation; in addition, its liberal and far-sighted policies presaged a fruitful development of art and decorative art there, and this counted for more than a little in the "Werkbund" assembly's choice.

By means of travelling exhibitions, the "German Museum for Art in Trade and Industry" seeks to encourage (or clarify) research in the domain of applied art.

Any city of more than 20,000 inhabitants can host these exhibitions, which show the best examples of every kind of object created for the mass market, with an emphasis on quality production and beautiful presentation. The archives of the museum are set up in such a way that exhibitions from a single department can be organised simultaneously in several cities.

The first event resulting from the efforts of the "Deutsches Museum" concerned the reform of printing, then of the poster, of wallpaper, of woven fabrics, and of small objects in metal and wood.

In the cities where the "Werkbund" and "The Union for the Education of the Merchant" had already offered conferences, these exhibitions provided a strong visual complement.

They were welcomed, in most cases, by Chambers of commerce, which installed them in their own facilities instead of allowing them to be exiled in the galleries of museums. This way, the merchant, the businessman or the industrialist could not fail to visit and to allow themselves to be convinced. In other cities these exhibitions were organised at the request of similar authorities or, occasionally, of private individuals. At the time of my visit to Mr Osthaus, director of this museum and proprietor of the "Folkwang" museum, it was proposed that I bring these exhibitions to our city.

Thus, an exhibition of "modern ceramics", an exhibition of "women's finery", an exhibition of "commercial printing and posters", etc., etc. will travel from place to place.

– Here are the conditions under which these exhibitions are organised: four cities, not far from each other, must cooperate and provide satisfactory premises free of charge. Each is required to pay 120 marks (in the case where the cooperation of four cities is not possible, the payment is 150 marks for only one city, 135 marks each for two or three cities). Once this is done, the "Deutsches Museum" defrays all other costs of transport, organisation, etc.

It sends its administrator, and places the necessary advertisements in the local journals; it insists that the cost of entry to the exhibition not exceed 50 centimes. In addition, it will furnish posters at a rate of 5 marks per hundred. The exhibition is strictly limited to modern works in order to produce the most lively, most effective presentation.

The museum also invites artists, industrialists, merchants to send whatever might relate to the topic of the exhibition. If the topic is printing or posters, for example, it will display ten examples. As compensation, the museum will send one selection, from among the items it has received, to each of its exhibitions, and, in this manner, it directs the attention of the public towards the artistic creator of the projects and towards his client. And in this way the collaborative ties between art and industry are always more firmly tightened.

In Berlin, I had the opportunity to visit the travelling exhibition called "Art in the Service of the Merchant", encompassing in this case everything that bears printed advertising. It had been organised at the request of one of the great houses of furnishings, which will be discussed later, the "Hohenzollernhaus", Bellevuestrasse (now Leipziger Strasse).

I saw everything in this exhibition which, incidentally, was very condensed and, because of this, singularly persuasive: boxes for sweets, prepared for the confectioners by the School of Decorative Arts in Vienna, in cardboard covered with gaily ornamented papers, framing a characteristic view from a great number of cities famous for their art: the "Zwinger" in Dresden, "Schönbrunn" in Vienna, "Am Wall" in Bremen, "Hradschin" in Prague. There were also various wrapping papers by the "Wiener-Werkstätte"; from these ateliers were exhibited packaging for the "Cida" brand of chocolate, for which the famous architect J. Hoffmann succeeded in creating small masterpieces of the genre (twelve different types). In a different gallery were displayed clippings, taken from German dailies, of manifestly artistic advertisements. Then there were cigarette packages, cigar boxes, etc., letterheads and envelopes for individuals and commercial enterprises, postcards, and the whole rich and often very beautiful procession of posters which, in these last few years, has assumed a deeply artistic character.

As the founder of the "Deutsches Museum" had fully anticipated, [mutual] interest brought to mind the clever artist who could make a work of art in such a modest frame, to the businessman or the manufacturer who could draw out a profitable product from this new tendency.

I conclude this study of the "Deutsches Museum" by mentioning the exhibition that I saw in Hagen, at the time of my visit to Mr Osthaus, which had been organised quickly by the tireless director, on the occasion of a convention of hairdressers in that city. A marvellous collection had been brought together: of articles of women's toilette and dress from the time of Egypt until the present; of drawings, rare engravings, showing the art of dressing one's hair across the ages; Mr Osthaus also resolved to entice the attendants of the convention there and to put together a small conference for them on the introduction of more artistry in women's hairdressing and in the articles of her toilette. He presented them a series of finished examples for their boutiques and their factories, such as: cases, perfume flasks, boxes for powder, for cream, combs, brushes, bracelets, necklaces and diadems, etc., etc.

"… All of this to allow the image of our age to assert itself still more strongly."

VERMITTLUNGSSTELLE FÜR ANGEWANDTE KUNST –
München
(Office for intervention in the applied arts, Munich)

Munich has thousands of artists. Life has been made difficult, in recent years, for the poet who varnishes canvases but forgets to sell them – or cannot – and it is no doubt largely this malaise that has suddenly given Munich a dominant position in the movement to renew the applied arts. Hundreds of artists there want to find a way out of the impasse. But how are these men who have lived entirely outside commercial and industrial life, how are they to get along with businessmen – clients – who, seizing the moment, want to use art for speculative aims?

When the movement for renewal came about, the creation of an "office of intervention" for the applied arts suggested itself. Munichois artists, architects, painters and sculptors had already formed an association. It was within their organisation that they based this new institution.

The task of the **"Office of intervention"** is to provide, in a very general way, information and advice on all artistic questions; its more particular goal is to procure tasteful and entirely suitable projects for whomever requests them; finally, through mutual influence and through negotiation or persuasion, it seeks the effective collaboration of artists and craftsmen, and in this way, **it seeks to perform an instructive function.**

Even if the artist were not directly associated with the organisation, it would still "intervene" on his behalf, whether he lives in Munich or in the surrounding area, or even abroad; in the latter case, always on the condition that he belongs to the "Association of Artists for the Applied Arts".

The intervention can take place for anyone: officials, private individuals, or societies, and it can involve individual efforts or the referral of work to a qualified workshop.

The office is organised as follows:

A director with necessary assistants. The director expedites correspondence, administration of funds, provides information, establishes protocol, and executes decisions of the Artistic Council.

The "Artistic Council" consists of four permanent members and four auxiliary members chosen from the body of the society for a one-year term. Every six months, half of their terms expire, although they are eligible for re-election. If possible, all the members of this Council belong to different artistic disciplines. Occasionally, the council may be supplemented by craftsmen who will play an advisory, but not a decisive, role.

The director and council members agree never to pursue their own interests.

The council considers all important events, approves expenditures, judges projects presented, recommends artists and verifies the competence of the director.

The "Office of Intervention" is not expected to provide income for the society.

The costs for the society occasioned by the creation of the "Office of Intervention" are defrayed through contributions of members, through a 5% commission deducted from the fee of artists, and through fees negotiated in advance with the client.

Advice is generally free. The management reserves the right, however, to charge a fee in certain instances.

Whenever possible, portfolios containing the work of artists, catalogues, samples, will be made available to anyone who requests them. However, these will not be handed over to interested parties unless they agree beforehand, in writing, not to make drawings, tracings or photographs of the projects included. Projects that must never leave the "Office for Intervention" must be marked accordingly.

All of the projects to be recommended will already have been approved by the "Artistic Council".

The activity of this office is impressive; the very courteous relations that I established with its director, Baron von Pechmann, during my stay in Munich, allowed me to see its great usefulness.

A manufacturer or a businessman wanting to promote himself with some pleasing advertisement, in some unfamiliar publication, no longer has to seek out an artist. Ill informed, he would encounter every possible setback, endless frustration and a loss of time, as one could well imagine. He goes to the "Office of Intervention", describes his ideas, his tastes, and the Director, who knows his discipline, knows how to play it like an instrument, will immediately identify the best man for the job, and a few days later, he will put the client in possession of what he desires.

The reach of this office enlarges daily thanks to a seemingly infinite network of relations. It is now possible for the "Office of Intervention" to undertake grand projects. Its role was therefore enormous during the great manifestation of applied arts by the Munichois at the "Salon d'Automne of Paris 1910".

It is now playing an equally considerable role in the organisation of the next "Munich Exhibition 1912", the study of which I take up next.

AUSSTELLUNG MÜNCHEN
(Munich Exhibition)

Munich has always enjoyed the good favour of foreigners; it is widely known as a city of art and a city with initiative. In the past few years, Munich, through an establishment called "Ausstellung München", has found a way to make the "dead season" a lively time of year during which hundreds of thousands of foreigners congregate. This institution includes a complete cycle of artistic solemnities involving music (Strauss week, Bruckner week, Mahler week, Wagner week, Brahms week, French Festivals, etc.), theatre with shows by the Théâtre des Artistes (Directed by Max Reinhardt) and finally the Applied Arts (exhibitions of furniture, of Islamic art, of Bavarian industry).

None of this takes place in anything but a deliberately modernist framework, and all the immense forces of art and enterprise in Munich are, thus, brought in to contribute.

The Exhibition is open from spring to autumn; Munich, as I have said, is inundated with foreigners.

It is evident that in this colossal enterprise, where all the interests of the decorative and industrial arts are at stake, the "Office of Intervention" and above all its director, Baron von Pechmann, have a considerable role to play. What follows is organisational information I received from the latter. We speak here especially of the new exhibition of 1912, which aspires to bring about great progress in the artistic composition and execution of freestanding furniture. The need for this became evident after the Munichois exhibition at the Salon d'Automne in Paris. The undertaking had been enormous. The Munichois expected a much-deserved triumph. It was nothing of the sort. They exhibited the rooms of a private mansion – vestibule, reception hall, salon, library, dining room, music room, Gentleman's bedroom and Lady's bedroom with bathrooms; their greatest architects had been assembled (Niemeyer, Bertsch, Emmanuel von Seidl, Bruno Paul, Veil, etc.) and their largest manufacturing houses guaranteed an irreproachable execution. The ensemble was strikingly harmonious, certainly very new for the French of today; but, as I emphasised at the beginning of this report, the Germans lack tradition, and their hands are still unskilled. The French thus found seemingly intolerable barbarism in their furniture, and the criticism was rather sharp. This then is the basis for the decision of the Committee of the Exhibition of 1912 to forbid all decoration of ensembles and to focus solely on freestanding furniture pieces, in order to concentrate all efforts this time on the prescribed theme.

A journal has been founded so as to prepare the public; Baron von Pechmann has been entrusted with editing.

The enterprise requires an enormous amount of capital, which is administered by a financial corporation created for this purpose. As for the rest, what follows is its basic organisation:

Four groups have been brought together:

1ˢᵗ   The Society of Applied Art (composed of members such as Prof. Theodor Fischer, Riemerschmid, Benno Becker, B. von Pechmann).

2ⁿᵈ   The Union of Decorative Arts, consisting of artisans (these two societies include members common to each).

3ʳᵈ   "Verein Ausstellung-Park", a financial enterprise.

4ᵗʰ   Society for the Preservation of Local Art.

And they have formed a fifth collective organisation responsible to, and noted in, the Trade register, the "Direktorium zur Abhaltung der Bayerischen Gewerbeschau 1912 in München".

Capital is guaranteed by the "3ʳᵈ" Society; the city and state are **providing** approximately half a million [marks].

The purpose of this impressive exhibition is not only to attract foreign tourists by making Munich an artistic and intellectual centre, but also to make Munich a commercial centre.

The intention of the organisers is to compete with the "Leipzig Trade Fair" or rather to provide overflow for it, since Leipzig is crowded and is no longer adequate. This, however, would be a selective exposition of all branches of art. It will seek to interest wholesalers from the United States and elsewhere. The programme has been drawn up by Prof. Theodor Fischer.

A lecture by Baron von Pechmann sought to explain that Munich could and should claim this place alongside Leipzig because of its art and its relative lack of industry (which is a protection for the industrial enterprises of Leipzig), because of the crowds of foreigners.

To this end, an Exhibition Park was constructed some years ago by the city, providing, each summer season, immense exhibition facilities fitted out with great taste. Around these buildings are found restaurants, cafés, the hall of music festivities, the Artists' Theatre and the Puppet Theatre (I will talk about these two theatres later). A vast park surrounds them. All of these buildings are grouped harmoniously, creating squares; their designs, produced by the most celebrated architects of Munich, seem to subordinate themselves to an idea of the whole. The use of reinforced concrete has, moreover, established new forms that, if they are not quite beautiful, are at least perfectly suitable.

Surrounding this whole affair is a huge and intelligently run advertising campaign. I have already said that the various societies are working together for the improvement of the applied arts. They therefore have their most meritorious artists, architects, painters, sculptors, designers, their most famous houses of furnishing, of lithography, of printing collaborate on their projects; this is evident in a magnificent performance hall, the Puppet Theatre by Paul Ludwig Troost, in the form of a model theatre (the Künstler-Theater) that marks a significant reform in the art of theatre production (which Parisians would surely recognise given to the models exhibited in the Salon d'Automne); in the form of restaurants inscribed with all the attractions of modernity; in the form of posters, of brochures, books, spread out for the whole world to see and all edited with care and a concern for beauty and modernism.

Even the subject of each exhibition is of inestimable educational value: in 1908, **the reform of furniture**; in 1910, **The Exhibition of Islamic Art** which presented visitors with the most extraordinary treasures in rugs, in brocades, in armours, in lacquers, in miniatures, in ceramics, etc.; that was certainly a unique event in the history of art exhibitions. In 1912 a decisive step will be made in the furniture industry.

The repercussions of such an enterprise on the life of the city will not take long to make themselves felt: during the summer of 1910 there was a revolution in the art of shop window displays; on the instigation of some grand enterprise that requested the assistance of an artist for the valorisation of its products, this lit a wildfire along the main roads, especially among the shops of the silk trade, of the confectioners, among the pastry shops, in the book shops, in the restaurants, etc. Luxurious hotels, which wanted to offer to their guests the same style that they came to admire at the exhibition, were built or remodelled. During the festivities, the decoration of the streets was no longer left in the hands of private individuals, but the grand arteries were given over to the architects and to the painters, who inspired unified works, marshalling all people of goodwill, without whom they would have exhausted themselves in sterile toil, under a shared vision of beauty.

Even daily dirigible flights in the Bavarian Alps were organised. And its gondola will soon be the work of a respected architect.

Thus one can conclude that in this city of Munich "all the successful reforms in education and the trades are intimately tied to life, accompany progress, and have a rational, practical significance."

All this has been, so far, a worthy collaboration among designers and producers.

It was also necessary to present the results to the public, so that it could see, critique, educate itself, and, in so doing, develop a fruitful response to the mechanisms of production. It was necessary to establish contact and mutual respect. The medium of the exhibition was certainly the most eloquent, the most direct for this. I had already begun to study the subject and, by studying the "Ausstellung München" organisation, have understood it much more fully.

I will not mention the exhibition of painting, which would divert me from my subject, but before reporting on several of the most significant of these manifestations of utilitarian art, I will underscore this point: it is that, as has already been mentioned, Germany is not a single entity. And each state dreams of realising what Munich has brought about. This is true of cities such as Dresden, which already appeal to popular taste; it is true of others such as Hamburg, such as Berlin, such as Düsseldorf, which scarcely ever do. They also have organised very special, very lively exhibitions; they have founded schools, on which they wish to confer a great lustre through the appointment of celebrated masters. The municipal sacrifices are enormous, and certainly this legitimate ambition has created conditions for very fruitful competition.

Berlin has taken the lead by displaying an almost unhealthy lust for growth. This city will soon be gigantic, and it will exemplify the modern city for the Old World. Some months' stay in this city have endeared it to me, while on the first visit, a year earlier, it seemed rather dreadful, disproportionate, inhumane.

In the exhibitions that it organises, it does not, like Munich, engender a good-natured charm – which would be impossible – but a craving for simplified grandeur, a desire to be the harbinger of the most modernist ideas; it pushes the principles of its utilitarian aims to their most transcendent consequences.

The titles of two considerable exhibitions that I visited in the spring of 1910 are indicative: "Die Allgemeine Städtebau-Austellung" (General Exhibition of the Art of Town Planning), "Die Ton-, Zement- und Kalkindustrie-Austellung" (Exhibition of the Clay, Cement and Lime Industries).

DIE ALLGEMEINE STÄDTEBAU-AUSSTELLUNG

was like a competition where all the theoreticians who have published so many abstruse books in recent years, so many utopian theories, who have called for and proposed so many improvements in the domain of the construction of cities, came to joust. The problem was posed a long time ago, because of the malaise of the great cities and of their ever more intrusive ugliness. The exhibition in Berlin, organised with an admirable breadth of outlook, showed the tremendous results already obtained almost everywhere, particularly in Germany. I will say that in Germany the efforts have been exclusively reformist, while in America it has been the increasingly formidable exploitation of their builders' genius, and that in France – which Paris alone embodies and represents – it has been the continuation of a tradition judged perfectly adequate and worthy of carrying on.

Instead of being asked to decipher arduous and ill-tempered scrawls, one had before one's eyes much more eloquent results or practical assertions. There were contradictions, shared tendencies, protestations, propositions, the struggle against the diagram, and the cliché of official administrations; it was on this subject that many cities triumphed, having transformed their city planning offices, and having renounced ancient development plans, they had appealed to celebrated architect–artists enlivened by a certain patriotic fire necessary in such circumstances; these cities proudly exhibited new, progressive plans, hoping thereby to distinguish themselves in the confederation of cities and to cover themselves with a certain glory (Munich, Cologne, Mannheim, Brunn, Gothenburg in Sweden, Nuremberg, Essen, Rostock, Stockholm, Copenhagen, Helsingsfors, Hanover, Darmstadt, Stuttgart, Posen, Aachen, Gdansk, Frankfurt, Königsberg).

There were even some who felt the need to confess their sins, and they lined up, side-by-side on the walls, the expansion projects shaped according to the laws of the routine in complete calm and satisfaction by the employees of city planning offices – and the new projects drawn up by architect–artists. The confession was touching, conclusive, and deep down did it not mix in some small grain of vanity or pride? In this way Cologne, Mannheim, Karlsruhe, Vienna, etc. expressed their pride.

The reform of cemeteries occupied a significant place of its own. Cremation, on one hand, and the atrocious ugliness achieved in this area during the last few years, simultaneously spurred an energetic reaction. Of the many guises the proposed reforms could have assumed, a severe regimentation was the point of departure for all of them, the only possible way. Here as well competitions or direct commissions had put the whole enterprise in the hands of celebrated architects (Laeuger, Schumacher, Behrens, Grässel, etc.).

The halls dedicated to the exhibition of cemeteries, with their projects for subdivision, for buildings (chapels, crematoria, columbaria), for the grouping of tombs, for types of tombs, etc., certainly revealed one of the most urgent tasks that the councillors of all cities have had to resolve.

I cannot, of course, tarry any longer on this crucial manifestation of art that is to be introduced in the city and its administration. I will say again that the impetus for it was the "Gross-Berlin" (Greater Berlin) competition, which required the provision of plans for the expansion of this city and proposals to make it the quintessential modern city.

The projects were exhibited in the hall of honour; it was huge, gigantic, impressive and perhaps even very beautiful. There one observed men now capable of confronting any problem. Berlin wants to be not only practical, hygienic, agreeable, but beautiful also, and there was in the proclamation of this challenge, which lasted several years, a little of that Florentine pride that could erect the dome of Santa Maria del Fiore.

It is clear that this exhibition was addressed to designers. Who has not seen visitors insensible to these mysterious drawings? I devoted several days of hard work there, in order to touch lightly upon the subject; it so happens that I was writing a study on the construction of cities, and these hours were profitable for me.

TON-, ZEMENT- UND KALKINDUSTRIE-AUSSTELLUNG

This was the grand introduction of the building industries to the architects and the engineers. The lesson was decisive; there was not an architect who did not return from this visit lost in thought or filled with enthusiasm – a great transformation in the elements of building is being made so as to shake up those who have learned to believe that because certain materials have been used for centuries they have become unchangeable, and to give new ideas to the dreamers, and great open fields to the men embarking on research into the path of modernism. An air of freedom was blowing there.

There were lectures being given at every moment. I heard the question of "Heimatschutz" raised in front of the united members of the "Werkbund" in response to the conflict between manufacturers of tiles and those of Eternit: the speaker demanded, so that the public could be set straight, that "Heimatschutz" declare that the sole protection for the fundamental value of ancient works was to discredit the so-called "archaeological" method and to march forward.

One manufacturer spoke about the crisis created by the fabricators of cement products who flood the market with new products, confounding the architects as to their application and the public as to their tastefulness. He concluded, citing Fridtjof Nansen: there is only one way: "Vorwärts!"

Another speaker posed this question: is art a fantasy that guides material, or is it material that dictates the form of art? He continued, concluding that the architect must not create forms and give them to the engineer, but he himself must discover the intimate possibilities of materials and know how to give them form and to employ them adequately. He showed reinforced concrete driving out iron and the coincidence of new materials with the act of creation. The visit to the exhibition which followed this speech was designed to dissipate any doubts about the radical transformation to the forms of architecture that will be dictated by new materials, which are more practical, more economical, more hygienic, incombustible, and, perhaps, just as beautiful when put to rational use.

If I have described these two exhibitions in Berlin with a few details it is to characterise their avant-garde tendencies effectively. I will now report, in the form of a list, other similar enterprises.

AUSSTELLUNG BEMALTER WOHNRÄUME –
München 1910
(Exhibition of painted rooms – Munich 1910)

This was intended to be a variation on the initiatives of the "Office of Intervention for Artistic Projects". Organised luxuriously enough by its patrons, commercial building painters, it sought to prove to the public that good taste and modern tendencies had made their way into corporations and that the public could henceforth call upon building painters and entrust them with everything involving interior decoration.

The very telling results proved once again that teaching should be left to those who have taught themselves; they retold the fable of the magpie who put on the feathers of the peacock. This exhibition has a role to play here; it illustrates a new side of an evolution that is too rapid and the danger of a speculative frame of mind poorly directed in the domain of art.

I saw the same exhibition six months later in Hamburg: **"Ausstellung Bemalter Räume"** (spring 1911). The results were infinitely more artistic than those of Munich; it had completely reversed direction. One needs only note the organisation on one hand (architect Prof. Meyer, director of the "Kunstgewerbeschule") and the exhibitors on the other, among whom I mention the "Vereinigte Werkstätten" with the architects

Bruno Paul and Schröder. Apart from generally successful halls exhibited by the large-scale producers of furniture showing the possible contribution of what could be called "house painting", the industrial firms exhibited new products, admirable lacquers for furniture, new stuccos, plastic coatings for floors, etc.

"Ethnographic Exhibition" at Wertheim (Wertheim, the celebrated department store of the "Leipziger Platz" in Berlin, lodged in a work of architecture by Messel, that still remains, for Germany, the quintessential luxury department store): this permanent exhibition, instituted under the auspices of the "Ethnographic Society", is a sales counter for all of the objects of European popular art. There one buys, at good prices, prestigious Czech, Romanian, Serbian and Bulgarian embroidery, thick Finnish tapestries, sculpted wood from Russia, pottery from all of Germany, from Bohemia, from Thoune, etc. and also Negro and Japanese basketry, etc. This is not merely a display of bric-a-brac but a selection of the finest examples. The success of this exhibition seemed to me to be very great.

. . . .

... and I will say etcetera, etcetera, since this means of contact between artists and the public has made the Germans, who were inspired by the Viennese, masters as far as exhibitions are concerned.

———————————

To study the repercussions of this great movement in the commercial and speculative world, repercussions that constantly revitalise the efforts of the "Werkbund", I will limit myself to a few significant cases. Here more than anywhere there are innumerable pages that one could write.

I will concentrate my remarks on two themes:

1st **ART IN THE SERVICE OF COMMERCE. "Vereinigte Werkstätten für angewandte Kunst". The case of the "A.E.G.". The reform of typography and the renovation of the book. Department stores and the "college of shop front design" founded by the "German Union for the education of the Merchant";**

2nd **ART IN SERVICE OF SPECULATION: the "Garden Cities".**

1ST

DEUTSCHE WERKSTÄTTEN and VEREINIGTE WERK-STÄTTEN FÜR ANGEWANDTE KUNST

(United Societies)

This is now the largest establishment for art production, spreading its activity from the construction of private mansions, interior decoration, furniture, wall hangings, wallpaper, lighting fixtures, fabrics and tapestries, ceramics, etc. to jewellery, to the curio, to the postcard. A reciprocal contract links it to the "Wiener Werkstätte" (architect Josef Hoffmann, painters Klimt, Kolo Moser, Löffler, Czeschka, etc.) a similar enterprise that was founded earlier in Vienna and whose impact is no less significant. I know the workings of the "Wiener Werkstätte" very well having been hired by the office of Josef Hoffmann; but I will limit myself to the study of the "Deutsche Werkstätten" since it is Germany that I study.

The "Deutsche Werkstätten" GmbH (Gesellschaft mit beschränkter Haftung. Limited liability corporation) is not based on publicly traded stocks but upon **shares** belonging to various interests, bankers, individuals or speculators; the directors hold significant shares.

The "Vereinigte Werkstätten" is a publicly traded company.

These two presently united organisations have joined forces. They will soon separate. They joined in the hope of forming a sort of "trust". But different commercial motives are bringing them to a break-up. The "Deutsche Werkstätten" have always worked for profit, sometimes resolving themselves to compromise in the interests of the consumer, whereas the "Vereinigte Werkstätten", not wanting to suffer losses due to an enormous advertising campaign, aim, through the richness and tastefulness of their products, to maintain themselves in the position of the avant-garde throughout Germany.

The companies have headquarters, factories and salesrooms in Munich, in Berlin, in Hamburg, in Bremen, in Cologne, in Hanover.

Artistic direction in Munich is entrusted to Mr Karl Bertsch, commercial direction to Director Schimon. Collaborators in the "Deutsche Werkstätten" are W. v. Beckerath, K. Bertsch, O. Gussmann, W. Kreis, A. Niemeyer, R. Riemerschmid, etc. Those of the other company: Bruno Paul, Em. v. Seidl, O. Krüger, R. A. Schröder, B. Pankok, Th. Th. Heine, Marg. v. Brauchitsch, E. Erler, E. Orlik, E. R. Weiss, etc.

In addition to these regular collaborations, the workshops are prepared to accept the work of other artists, provided that it is tasteful enough not to compromise the reputation they have established.

If one were to stay in Germany for a while, one would feel the power of this cooperation among artists recruited in the interests of fruitful speculation. One can say that their shops are admirable. They always consist of numerous shop fronts open at the "strategic points" of a city. One cannot avoid them, since they inevitably occupy the luxurious quarters and the thoroughfares frequented by foreigners (in Munich, Odeonsplatz; in Berlin, Bellevuestrasse; in Bremen, Am Wall, etc.). The cost of entry is free and there is no obligation to purchase. One enters into them just as easily as into the dealers of paintings by Druet, Bernheim, Durand-Rueil, etc. in Paris. The ground floor is full of cases in which are displayed a thousand curios, jewels, ivories, embroideries, of rugs, tapestries, fabrics of all sorts, pieces of furniture, ceramics, etc. I add that the whole arrangement from top to bottom is made with perfect taste, whether by Bertsch in Munich or by Paul in Berlin and in Bremen.

Richly printed and illustrated catalogues (quintessential examples of the genre) displayed on the tables are at the disposal of visitors. One or more floor levels consist of a diverse succession of rooms for sale, or of model rooms built up over several years, each following the designs of one artist, and in which are displayed all of the modern experiments and trends. The conception is unified, the effect irresistible. Parisians can remain sceptical as to their taste, on account of the incompatibility of the two races, which seems to be pronounced here, where everything that offers itself to the eyes is in some way the expression of the German soul; but these Parisians, if they do not admire everything, are at least impressed by the harmony, which is undeniable. From the curtains, the fabrics, the furniture, the rugs, the lighting fixtures, the dishes, the curios, everything is born of the same desire finally to realise compatibility, proportion, affinity, **kinship**. I have said that this was eminently harmonious; having recognised this, the critic can then put it into practice.

Either one of these rooms is bought en bloc by an individual or the model is reproduced for him. In any case, at the end of one, two or three years the rooms are dismantled and others are rebuilt.

Thus the visitor passes from a salon, to a dining room, to a boudoir, to a bedroom, to a reception room, as if some rich owner is presenting him the pleasures of his mansion.

I had tolerable relations with the directors of the Society in Munich, to whom I presented objects that the Ateliers d'Art had sent me. It was not an unfruitful move. Many things interested directors Bertsch and Schimon, Baron v. Pechmann, Mr Riemerschmid, and Prof. Theo. Fischer, and I maintain the hope of a possible collaboration. I then visited the factories of Munich and Hellerau, near Dresden, where furniture, embroideries, tapestries and lighting fixtures are made.

The latter is set up in the midst of a splendid landscape. The architect Riemerschmid was wise enough not to make a blight of these utilitarian buildings. It is around this very factory that the astonishing city of Hellerau, of which I will speak later, has begun to develop. In order to describe the importance of this factory, answerable to the "Deutsche Werkstätten", it will suffice if I mention its warehouses, container of more than one million marks' worth of wood (ebony, mahogany, etc.).

Apprentices are trained in a very intelligent way there. Up to ten apprentice carpenters, for example, have one workman as a master. From the beginning they make **useful and saleable items**, boxes, stools, etc. then increasingly complicated items, always for sale. The apprenticeship costs 800 marks and lasts three years. They have a drafting room where they draw from nature and practise construction.

The equipment of the factory is exemplary. Some of the machines are astonishing. An incredible cleanliness reigns everywhere; a pipe of 10, 15 or 20 cm appended to each machine serves as a vacuum, that is to say it removes all of the dust and sawdust from the moment it is produced; only the scraps remain; every evening these are pushed to the foot of a wall, towards an opening communicating with a suction pump that removes them and transports them immediately into a furnace.

No designs are created at the factory; the artists furnish projects free of charge (Riemerschmid, Niemeyer, Bertsch) but they receive one per cent on the sale of each piece, the total number of which could be unlimited. Models are displayed by affiliates where they are described and advertised to the public in catalogues and brochures. Thus everyone profits as if he were his own salesman, without loss of time, however, in fabrication or in sales. Once again there is shrewd understanding.

Today Germany boasts a multitude of these great furniture manufacturers. **"Ballin"** in Munich (designs by P.-L. Troost, etc.), **"Saalecker-Werkstätten"** (architect Schultze-Naumburg, the author of the eloquent works on Heimatschutz), **"Hohenzollern-Kunstgewerbehaus"** and **"Keller und Reimer"** in Berlin (designs by

Peter Behrens, Grenander, Alwin Müller, Pankok, etc.). The latter organises lectures on the problem of interior decoration in its premises.

THE CASE OF A.E.G.
"Allgemeine Elektricitäts Gesellschaft"

I do not know the origins of this colossal enterprise that employs 60,000 workers in its factories. I visited the factories with the "Werkbund" in June 1910; then I had the opportunity, during my internship of five months with Peter Behrens, to get to know some of aspects of the company that are relevant to this study.

AEG provides electrical machines, light bulbs, and parts for electrical devices to the entire world. The board of directors has found a way of exploiting the reform movement asserting itself in architecture, by imprinting its consumer goods with a character of perfect convenience ruled by the laws of taste – so as to generate competition, which all architects want, with the deplorably ornamented hardware of stamped metal or of cast brass that, under the pretext of decoration, continues to encumber lighting fixtures, cooking stoves, even machines. In addition, meters, gauges, and other objects too numerous to mention, brought their leprous stains into homes and disfigured the halls of machines as well. The board searched out the man who could develop the perfectly adequate, perfectly proportioned form, the form perfectly suited to the inherent qualities of materials.

It chose **Peter Behrens**, and named him **Artistic Advisor of AEG**. Since then it has been possible to admire power stations which are works of architecture inseparable from our age – facilities with composure and admirable cleanness, in the midst of which superb machines add a serious and imposing note. Since then, also, electric lamps, electric switches, contacts, electric cooking stoves, numerous fixtures for heating and lighting demanded by modern comfort, have taken on a modest, sober, **almost impersonal** appearance. They are discreet witnesses, while formerly they disfigured. Because Peter Behrens designed all of their forms, there is not one visible aspect of the building construction or of the production coming out of AEG that has not been reworked by him.

The success of this authoritarian intervention of art could have been deplorable had it not been entrusted to precisely the right man.

177

But the role of Peter Behrens does not stop there: all the new factories that arise in the ceaseless growth of AEG are in his hand. And the critics are unanimous in praising him. One even called his most recent factory, the "Turbinen-Halle", a "Kathedrale der Arbeit".

He built the extensive worker communities that will eventually house the more than 150,000 souls who earn their bread at AEG. Behrens is the profound, powerful, serious, staggeringly dominant force, who is not only suited to this task at this moment, but also to the contemporary German spirit.

THE REFORM OF TYPEFACES
THE RENEWAL OF THE BOOK

Germany is a country of bookshops. There, more than anywhere else, the book has assumed the crass ornaments and bad taste that attest to the great vainglories of the post-war era. Reform was preached in England under Ruskin and realised by William Morris. Germany has attended to the problem in recent years. I have already mentioned the efforts of the "Deutsches Museum" reaching out to support private initiatives. The brothers Klingspor of Offenbach, near Frankfurt, commissioned Peter Behrens to develop a complete alphabet with many punctuation marks and tailpieces suitable for innumerable combinations. At about the same time, two or three other artists were dealing with the same problem: Tiemann, E. R. Weiss and Ehmcke created fundamentally different typefaces, although all were inspired by a return to the beautiful Latin tradition. Most books in Germany have since been printed with these various typefaces.

The art of page layout, of paper manufacturing, of binding each underwent a similar reform.

In 1909, at the request of the state, Behrens gave a three-week course in his own office to some of its representatives. The goal of this course was the reform of script for placards, notices, bookplates, etc.

Since then, the display windows of certain bookshops in Germany have offered a captivating appearance that would be impossible to find in France. Booksellers have even become passionate about their trade, "about their art", they say. I met one in Düsseldorf who dug up treasures for me in the inner sanctums of his shop. He caressed them lovingly as if they were ancient manuscripts; they were "unicums", or limited

editions for collectors: because the rebirth of the book has aroused passionate biblio-
philes on the lookout for any new artistic creation.

Finally **"the department stores"**, similar to the "Louvre" or to the "Bon Marché"
in Paris, have entered into this outburst of beauty in Germany.

They are practically ideal for it. They are worlds where one can find anything:
Wertheim has promised to procure a living whale for whomever requests one – in a
fixed amount of time! To attract the client with the seduction of comfort, of luxury, of
beauty, to open its doors to the crowds that surge in, to display beautiful materials in
excessive detail, that is to say, to put them in the hands of the onlooker so that he
receives some physical impression, a sensual contact, to intoxicate him, and to tempt
him – that is the new tactic of the merchant.

Astonishingly tasteful window displays in the most intense centres of life arrest
the hurried crowds. The doors are actually heavenly portals. There are free elevators;
the complete neutrality of the salesmen never makes one feel pressured.

But, so that this often fantastic display in immense Halls flooded with light never
becomes wearisome as in an Oriental bazaar, it needed an order, an organisation, a
rhythm, a feeling for colour; the exploitation of decorative resources inherent to merchandise needed tact, taste – style if you will – **the art of display**.

This is a completely new art, only a few years old. It is developing with stunning
rapidity. Last winter in Berlin I saw shop fronts that one never tired of contemplating,
and I learned that at Wertheim, the painter Madame X creates a new harmony nearly
every week. It has to be the same at KaDeWe ("Kaufhaus des Westens").

What lies behind the indisputable success of all this is that the merchants, on the
occasion of the great competition of shop fronts organised by the city of Berlin in
1909, and on the advice of the "Werkbund", decided to establish a "College of Art
and Decoration" (in German the word "decoration", "decorator" designates the art
of display and the person who attends to window displays).

According to the merchants, the crowds associated with this competition were
comparable only to those of the Christmas season, which affirms the practical success
of the manifestation of taste in shop displays.

The directors of the **"Höhere Schule für Dekorationskunst GmbH"** undertake
commissions of all sorts, which they present to students as problems and practical
exercises for them to complete: table decorations (for receptions, etc.), holiday deco-

rations for homes, as well as even grander decorations (lights, decorations for mourning, street decorations), arrangement of pavilions and of whole exhibitions. Likewise, the school creates travelling exhibitions, which take place during the opening celebrations of new firms or at the seasonal exhibitions. In this way students are given the opportunity to make direct contact with good firms. There is an office of intervention for the receipt and awarding of commissions.

The teaching of the school consists of:

1ˢᵗ Design of plans and elevations, architectural design, and sketches of decoration. 2ⁿᵈ Study of colour (with practical exercises). 3ʳᵈ Study of styles (with slide projections). 4ᵗʰ Science of lighting (with practical demonstration of different sorts of lighting and their artistic significance).

Section B: 1ˢᵗ Painting of posters and signs. 2ⁿᵈ Carpentry and tapestry (with a focus on decoration). 3ʳᵈ Exercises in every sort of decoration. 4ᵗʰ Practical exercises in the styles and general issues concerning decorative art (interiors, individual rooms in shops, museums, exhibitions).

Students are regularly engaged in the decoration of display windows for the best stores in Berlin.

For employees already having knowledge of the trade, courses last two months; for beginners, six months. A new course begins each month. Tuition is 200 marks for two months, 75 marks for each additional month. – Free Employment Agency – Information and brochure at "Verband Berliner Spezialgeschäfte", Berlin W. 8, Leipziger Strasse 111.

Reading this curriculum it is truly bewildering to reflect on what has been, and what still is in many cities, the "art" of merchandise display.

2ᴺᴰ

ART IN SERVICE OF SPECULATION
GARDEN CITIES

Work in the city and live in the countryside, everywhere people do this more and more, and not only among the aristocratic class, but also in the middle class, and already among some in the working class. This has required immense speculation and a new organisation. The garden city is not new; it came from England. Until recently it has been content simply to be practical and beautiful according to the tastes of each individual. Today in Germany it needs to be beautiful **as a whole**; it needs to be harmonious, built in a unique style and precisely in that style and with that ease which have become so successful among the very rich classes. The great speculative enterprises offer, not far from the big city, completely charming little towns, made up of villas or of houses that look like villas, conceived in a taste that is sober, utilitarian and conven- ient. This, then, is a democratisation of the architecture of private mansions, putting it in reach of the masses and pandering to their desire to show off. Now the fashion follows modern works by Fischer, by Behrens and by Paul. The garden cities of greater Berlin, for example, put on these garments; the cut is not hideous, it is just that the cloth is less fine. Incidentally this effort is very laudable and its results show progress.

I have mentioned the tremendous growth of Berlin, to which the participation of greater Berlin will give an even greater vigour. The speculators, profiting from the spirit of the moment, have little by little laid their hands on favourable land, have established bold organisations whose goal is nothing less than the construction of towns dotted here and there along a railway line. Sometimes the railway is built from scratch; sometimes the stations are simply inserted between two points separated by nearly uninhabited wastelands. The rail service is admirably organised. The stations, which are always situated at the heart of the community, whose streets all radiate into the surroundings, are connected daily to the city by 100 or 200 trains. The price of the trip varies from 20 to 40 Pf. for 3rd class, from 30 to 69 Pf. for 2nd class. And the con- nections are so well set up that one often reaches these communities, some of which are very distant, more rapidly than the immediate suburbs of Berlin, Schöneberg, Friedenau, which are connected to the city by ordinary streetcars.

These new cities make up the garden cities.

What incites me to speak about them in this report is that in Germany, the aes- thetic inclination is founded as much on snobbery, the bourgeois spirit of imitation, as on a true revival of taste. The result of this is that the nouveau-riches and the bourgeois and all those who want to ape them, even when this would do them violence, want to live in the country, want to have luxurious villas in the taste of the moment, apartments not bought from a "Warenhaus", but conceived for them by fashionable artists.

And the speculative companies, considering this a normal manifestation of progress, are in complete agreement. This was one of their cleverest ideas.

Now all the brochures speak about beauty, about harmony, about good taste, about novelty. They flaunt the artist appointed supervisor of construction, or sometimes sole building contractor. The companies organised competitions or chose some famous man to draw up the street plan for the future city; because it is there more than anywhere else that one wants to use the newest formulas. The exhibition of the "Städtebau-Ausstellung" showed decisively the revolutionary tendencies in the construction of cities. The streets will be like the avenues of parks; they will curve for the best utilisation of the terrain. The stations will be charming in their fitness, and the large green spaces jealously guarded. The houses will be by Muthesius or by Bruno Paul or by Behrens or by one of their many satellites. So that, strolling on a spring or summer evening in the least significant of these cities, the visitor who comes from the great furnace of Berlin will be profoundly shocked; he will imagine himself living truly in the midst of a wholesome tranquillity.

A healthy, prosperous life takes shape among streets marked out for the repose of the eyes. He will sense that in ten years admirable things will be made of these garden cities, and he will calculate the inevitable effects of this new life in the country on the members of his family; then he will think about the incomplete joys of the big city, so strongly mixed with dissonance: exhibitions of painting, concerts, the worn-out symphonies and the opera. He will think of them as a kind of mistake, like something that cannot possibly go on. He will feel the necessity of a more domestic, more familial culture. And looking around himself, he will understand what these first great festivals are heralding for the future, where in **the most favourable circumstances, it is permissible for a soul to reveal itself, for artists to make almost total works of art:** music series, theatre series – "Munich-Ausstellung" with its Mahler festivals, its French festivals, its "Künstler-Theater", etc. – theatres à la Mézières and who knows, this rhythm of Jaques-Dalcroze, which one of the most eminent German social economists (an old man nevertheless) told me will surely make itself felt in social life.

Do I dream when I say this? These things, I have sensed them in all of the garden cities, in Munich, in Hagen, in Stuttgart, in Berlin. I felt it almost as a reality several months later in Hellerau, near Dresden.

It gave an even more astonishing impression than anywhere else. There a city was created from the ground up, solely by the greatest artists of Germany: Tessenow,

Muthesius, Riemerschmid, Baillie-Scott (England), Th. Fischer, Bestelmeyer, etc. Its inhabitants were first the factory workers of the "Deutsche Werkstätte für Handwerkskunst" (of which I have spoken), then a host of others. Two organisations are responsible: the directing organisation, "Gartenstadt-Hellerau", had acquired an immense, beautifully situated piece of land; it permitted anyone who wanted to build there, but under its direction; and, when I mention that this direction is under the acting Director of the "Werkbund", one will understand how significant this is. This company sells the land to the organisation named "Baugesellschaft-Hellerau", which builds the workers' houses designed by Tessenow, Riemerschmid, Muthesius, etc. – and I would be saying nothing if I did not add that this immense enterprise is founded on the following, which signals an advancement in social economy: **these two companies do not realise any profit above 4%; everything in excess of this quantity is applied to the improvement of the whole. The workers possess their houses by the sole fact that they pay their rent** – they possess them for thirty years, after which they can, at their discretion and without change of conditions, sign another thirty-year lease. In instances of misconduct, they will be evicted like ordinary tenants.

The workers are the owners of the company, since to be a tenant it is necessary to take part in the company, and one takes part in it by purchasing a share of 200 marks, payable in weekly instalments of 50 pfennigs or monthly instalments of 3 marks.

If they would like to raise or lower their rent, or make any modification, they decide on this themselves in a general assembly. – Hellerau is actually a cooperative. It diverts capital, usually directed to selfish ends, back to those who produced it. Hellerau seeks to become a centre of education, and it was for this reason, to begin with, that Jaques-Dalcroze, for whom the "Rhythmus GmbH" company was founded, was enticed there. The great institute has been built. Students, artists, teachers converge there from all parts of Europe. This is good. But what is better, is that all the children born in Hellerau will be educated by the Institute. (I have not, unfortunately, had time to study this last institution; I must content myself to write what others have told me.)

But I did stay in Hellerau, and as I have said, I believe that I have seen realised – or almost realised – the ideas that the communities of Berlin had suggested to me. Every year, in summer, festivals of rhythmic music, advertised in every corner of the globe, take place in the new theatre, stadium and palaestra that stands upon the eminence dominating Hellerau. Hellerau has become the director's seat of the "Werkbund".

To complete this chapter on garden cities, I will mention the one founded by the patron Osthaus, director of the "Deutsches Museum" and proprietor of the "Museum Folkwang".

Mr Osthaus never ceases to extol beauty by every possible means. To do this, he has designated a vast site for a garden city, superbly situated not far from Hagen. He has divided it into three contiguous parcels, which he has given to three architects whom he judges to be the greatest of the age: Josef Hoffmann, Vienna; Henry van de Velde, Weimar; Peter Behrens, Berlin. And each of these three leaders of the movement, masters of their domains, have drawn up designs for the streets and will raise up, little by little, a city that the patron wants to inscribe in history as a document of the age.

I could likewise mention a number of other communities, whose construction has been entrusted to artists of the first order. But what I have said on this matter suffices to demonstrate a characteristic method of using art, putting it in the service of the speculator and sometimes also of a higher cause.

THE REPERCUSSIONS OF THE POPULARISATION OF THE ARTS IN THE PUBLIC DOMAIN – THE OFFICIAL INITIATIVES

Since everything has been submerged or overthrown by new ideas, municipalities cannot have remained indifferent. And one can see this: official administrations, until recently sanctuaries of the routine, have allowed themselves, little by little, to overcome, act upon, repudiate obsolete practices and to place themselves squarely in the field of progressive action.

I will mention a few cases; the "General Exhibition of the Construction of Cities" supplies the most convincing evidence.

I have already said that some cities, Berlin and Munich especially, have sought to react against so-called "American" ugliness, having overturned their planning departments and inaugurated new processes. I have mentioned the consequences of this movement in other cities of the empire, which vividly proclaim their conversion by exhibiting expansion projects created by anonymous bureaucrats alongside those developed by the gifted artist they have chosen. This last fact marks a first step, an immense step, especially considering what still pretends to be unchangeable and infallible in so many cities: the planning bureaucracy. Some municipalities have gone a long way. They have, like Ulm's, sought to suppress building speculation by purchasing nearly all of the suburban land around the city, so that the land will continue to be affordable, and working-class garden cities can be developed easily there.

Municipalities used to have their accredited architects, and it was clear (the results show it) that they almost always personified the reaction against modernist ideas, and what is more, often cornered the market in bad taste. But now cities such as Munich show their self-respect with a University inaugurated in 1910 and built by Bestelmeyer. This is certainly the very finest achievement in the genre, marking an immense step forward. Beauty allies itself with convenience; the grand, sober lines dominate, and the crowd of students there gradually acquire, despite themselves, by osmosis, the taste for a calm, salutary beauty that is never obtrusive.

The University of Jena, built by Theodor Fischer, harmonises perfectly with the little town and the rustic hills that surround it. There is no longer the heavy solemnity that Bestelmeyer deemed necessary in the classical setting of the "Ludwigsstrasse". Here, everything has a more elegant, small-town feel; and, as is his habit, Theodor Fischer sought, with its decoration, to make a didactic work of modernism. He entrusted this to Ferdinand Hodler and to Ludwig von Hofmann.

Berlin, where buildings in any way symbolic are concerned, feels the stamp of its emperor weighing heavily upon it. And the new university under construction (Unter den Linden) will be in the same family as the Dome and the Reichstag building. It will be a testament to the violent struggle between the progressives and the reactionaries taking place there.

While visiting Jena, I noted the very touching sentiment of an alumnus who had raised a fountain in the corner of the court, at his own expense, in memory of his agreeable years at the university. A dedication commemorated him, and this fountain joined its sweet sentiment to the affability of Fischer's walls, making the university shimmer like a benevolent spirit over this little town nestled in the forest.

The entry of **responsible artists** into the administrative offices of the cities of Germany earned Dresden, for example, its new city hall and its famous slaughterhouses (architect Erlwein); for Hamburg, its popular park (under construction, architect Fritz Schumacher); for Berlin, the impressive streets of West Berlin where trams run amidst clipped lawns and beds of flowers between avenues of trees; for Stuttgart the reconstruction of an old quarter; for Munich four new cemeteries, celebrated ever since (architect Grässel), modern markets (under construction, architect Bertsch), etc. etc.

It would be good to point out the new cemeteries of Munich to the authorities: the West, the East, the North and the Wald-Friedhof. They, along with one in Hamburg, signal a completely new tendency: the cemetery wrested from its ugliness thanks to effective regulations and the authority of artists.

And art has made its way back into domains most frequently abandoned by it, in train stations, of which Hamburg offers the most remarkable example, in schools (those of Fischer in Stuttgart and in Munich, those of Ludwig Hoffmann in Berlin, which I saw impressively ornamented with flowers in the summer of 1910), even in the tunnels of the Metro of Berlin, etc., etc. While travelling through Saxony, I even noticed forest cuttings made with taste. Instead of mowing down whole forests, which is the custom in land reclamation, trees are left to stand in avenues and in harmonious groupings. I noticed the same done in the garden city district of Berlin.

Finally, since art was gradually taking control of official structures, increased taste in the conservation of ancient works had to follow. Munich is restoring its old churches in a most remarkable manner, demonstrating a modern, and not a timidly archaeological, spirit. Then cities like Frankfurt ("Verein für Heimatschutz"), Cologne and Dresden commissioned a young photographer, Miss Susanne Hoffmann-Darmstadt, to publish, on postcards, complete collections of notable works of architecture in their cities, mainly those that have been ignored. This is a form of propaganda without fanfare, which every city witnessing its artistic patrimony collapse under the claws of speculators would do well to employ.

It seems to me that it would be a good time to mention, at the end of this study, the "Werkbund's" manifesto concerning **the edict of the Prussian Ministry of Public Planning on the use of "State funds".**

This edict, published by the royal authorities of Prussia on the 1st of August 1908, concerned the use of State revenues; most of it consisted of important regulations on "State-funded construction projects".

Now, considering that among the allocations of the treasurer of the Office of Public Planning the art of building does not occupy the most insignificant place, and considering also **"that construction, whether it be public or private, is directly dependent on the applied arts"**, the "Werkbund" considered the occasion favourable for joining in the debate opened by the edict of the minister, and published the manifesto whose contents are summarised here:

An economy guided by a perfect sense for art and technique does not build up any obstacle to the manifestation of art. Nothing has done more harm to building in these last decades than the abuse of exterior ornamentation. It is not necessary to go far to find proof of this: there is an abundance of structures rising everywhere about which one could say: "Too bad the architect had so much money at his disposal!" As paradoxical as this might sound, one could add: "The richer the décor, the less its effect signals progress for art." This is not true of any particular class of art; it is a fact inherent to all art, inherent to the artist.

The artistic impression of an edifice does not rest solely in its display of exterior decoration, which, incidentally, is nothing but a matter of style, but above all in the expression of its form born of programme and of technical necessities and resting upon the complete satisfaction of the needs of the age. The architect must therefore possess absolutely thorough knowledge of modern progress; he should be familiar with new materials whose use always makes his work more suitable, always more useful, and usually more economical. So that the architect can achieve the most refined level of beauty with the most minimal means, he needs to have a profound understanding of the different branches of the building industry, building materials, their use and their handling, their price.

Now, the greatest obstacle to the utilisation of the capacities and the forces of initiative is in their administration (in this particular case), in the bureaucratic indoctrination that is almost commonplace and which, unfortunately, results in the application of conventional systems. Everyone knows that these systems allow each employee to protect himself and to shirk responsibility. This miserable state of affairs is aggravated moreover by an intensive centralisation that puts obstacles in the way of every employee's personal initiative.

On the other hand, the administrative heads of the offices of public planning, if they are excellent administrators, are generally laymen where construction is concerned, and they are no more artists than they are technicians. Now, in this matter, some authority is needed; **this is why the "Werkbund" expresses the desire that in all cases, large construction projects be given only to transcendent architects, even if every indifferent administrator existed merely to prevent this from happening.**

In addition, it must be decreed in every official bureau of public planning, that the author of a project be made responsible for it and that his responsibilities be announced publicly. The logical and fruitful application of public revenue **should not lead to the restriction of the building artist** merely to give all the power to someone who knows how to "economise", so to speak, but who knows **nothing about the art of building.**

Thus, as the edict of the minister of Public Planning foretold, since an edifice (official edifices in this particular case) must first of all captivate the imagination through simplicity and vigour, through the harmony of masses and of contour, through the healthy organism which brings different elements to life, more than through costly materials and the multiplicity of exterior ornamentation, we will seek to skimp on superfluous decoration, but never on the artist. **Because the more restricted the available capital will become, the more it will be necessary to ensure the collaboration of a total artist to whom, moreover, we can entrust complete responsibility.** A comprehensive and weighty responsibility is not only a stimulant, but it is a guarantee of success, since it summons all the active capabilities of the one who is the object of it. Thus the edict of the Minister of Public Planning would serve to bring about the most advantageous effects, if, leaving aside this necessity to economise, the consequences were drawn out to their logical conclusion: **to gather the forces that are in a position to achieve the most perfect results with the most modest means.**

I could go on and on enumerating the thousand repercussions provoked by the placement of art in service of commerce, of industry and of public life in Germany. I end this account here, closing it with the quotation from the beginning: **The Germans having become conscious of their artistic physiognomy are attempting bring themselves into balance through the effort of artists and tradesmen, who, each gravitating to his proper station, lend each other mutual support.**

III

TEACHING

TEACHING

THERE used to be Fine Arts academies in almost every provincial capital. There were secondary technical schools where architecture was taught. In the former, there was the perpetuation of the painting of Munich, Düsseldorf or Karlsruhe, in the latter, there was the formation of hundreds of young architects who, with a complete ignorance of art, with good faith at times, but frequently also with contempt for the discipline, were compelled to multiply the architectural forms of the decadent close of the 19th century. Certainly, this was lamentable, intolerable. The creation of new schools committed to the industrial arts, then to interior architecture, and finally to architecture proper, was bound to divert a part of the torrent of youthful energy engulfed until then in the "Hochschulen".

A school is a school, and the work of the pupils often betrays little more than an imitation, more or less well understood, of the thoughts of their teacher. All reflects therefore the worth of the teacher, and it is this that makes the German schools of today so interesting. It is evident that pupils submitting to the influence of Fischer, van de Velde, Hoffmann, Behrens, Paul, Kreis or Pankok are apt to become at times important personalities, and in all cases the most capable producers of their day.

Among the many "Kunstgewerbeschulen" in Germany, I have visited those on which certain famous personalities have made a mark; those of Munich, Weimar, Hamburg, Düsseldorf, Berlin; I added, as a matter of interest, those of Dresden and Hanau.

Of course, I will not formulate criticism here, since this would be only personal. I will pass rapidly to the examination of various schools that I have visited, relaying only information that could be of some use. As we will see, all the eminent schools act according to this new pedagogical principle: not to make school a prison, but **a place where the student exercises his imagination.** And the way to attain this result is to think of the student as a man, to allow him full liberty as well as full responsibility.

These schools, founded in order to accompany the reform movement that has developed in the applied arts, have had to call upon the reformers. They have therefore recruited artists of this generation, that is to say that all the professors are young men and that many of them have not yet reached the age of thirty.

LEHR- und VERSUCHS-ATELIERS
für ANGEWANDTE und FREIE KUNST
Director Mr Wilhelm von Debschitz
(Debschitz School – Munich)

This is a private school that has the reputation for being the best in Germany.

Initial instruction involves the general education of taste; this is followed by the development of ornamental sensibilities; finally, each student is pushed to pursue his own talents in branches of art that best suit him. These include the various decorative arts trades and lead, for especially gifted students, to interior architecture.

Mr W. v. Debschitz teaches the artistic part himself. He is grooming a young man to succeed him, a former student, Mr Fritz Schmoll v. Eisenwerth.

Efforts are concentrated on research into Ornament. – For [work in] metal, ceramics and lace, special masters support the director, but they confine themselves to the teaching of technique. – The evening is given over to courses for figure drawing and modelling. Mr Debschitz provides criticism once a week in each class.

The school includes approximately 100 pupils; at one time it had 260 – which was too many. The director and owner, assisted by a secretary, assumes administrative responsibilities.

The school is lodged in a building facing on to a courtyard built for industrial workshops; thus the premises have turned out to be perfectly suitable. The installation is very basic. The furniture is worn, and the premises tell, with their dirty walls, of the work that goes on there. In the composition classroom several display cases protect collections of beetles, birds, small animals, etc.

Throughout the week the students execute all kinds of work, in workshops installed especially for the purpose: ceramic (statuettes, vases, curios, etc.), turned and sculpted wood (statuettes, confectionery boxes, cases for powder, for gloves, etc.), metal (dishes, lamps, damascening, jewellery, work in gold and silver), projects for furniture and for complete interior decoration. The furniture is not executed by the students; these projects are only introduced so as to produce clever designers. The execution, on the other hand, is never entrusted to a large firm, such as the "Deutsche Werkstätte" or "Ballin", but to small carpenters, men trained step by step by Mr Debschitz, and who have bound themselves to him by contract. They can, on occasion, undertake other work, but they are not permitted to refuse requests from the school.

Mr W. v. Debschitz acts very paternally towards his students. He encourages them particularly to play sports, asserting that health and good humour are excellent accompaniments to an artistic vocation. For this, he has founded clubs for tennis, for swimming and boating in his school, and makes a house on the shore of Lake Starnberg, in the Alps, available to the students where they can go to pass their Sundays devoting themselves to sport.

The students of Mr Debschitz thus develop themselves in every respect, producing designers who excel in everything that concerns applied art. A group of students has even founded a lace workshop in the mountains of the Schlesien Hirschberg; the populace that was already devoted to this work has become associated with the movement. On the basis of new ideas, this industry has been given new life.

LEHR- und VERSUCHS-WERKSTÄTTE – STUTTGART
Director Mr Bernhard Pankok
(workshops for teaching and research)

The director showed me the principal halls of the school; these are installed without luxury, similar to those of Mr Debschitz, in an old penitentiary. But here the prevailing tendency is to make "worker-artists" rather than "artist-workers".

The school is generally influenced by the teaching of Mr Pankok, although he is only involved with one of the following four sections:

1st Carpentry (Prof. Pankok). 2nd Ceramics (Prof. Rochga). 3rd Metal. 4th The art of the book (Prof. Cissach).

Workshop hours are broadly distributed in the programme. Each section has an artistic director and a master-technician.

The students, numbering approximately 80, can undertake work of their own, as long as they pay for their tools and the hours of machine operation. This work thus allows good students (or at least those who like the work) to pay for almost all of their tuition. A salesroom in one of the department stores on the Königstrasse is always at the disposal of students.

Each year a certain number of scholarships, supplied by the proceeds of special funds, are distributed as rewards to the top students. The students also take part in various open competitions in Germany and sometimes receive awards.

The most decisive results appeared to me to have been obtained in the carpentry class, which is, among all of the decorative art schools in Germany, the one that best follows the development of students' manual technique. The workshops are vast, the machines numerous.

KUNSTGEWERBESCHULE – DÜSSELDORF
(visit guided by Director Prof. Wilhelm Kreis)

Preparatory classes encompassing three semesters or more greet the young students; they are taught to see, not through tiresome drawing of plaster casts, but through drawing or water colouring from nature (still lifes). This pushes them little by little to devise tasteful layouts and to give them a sense of rhythm, to make colour choices, to develop an artistic personality.

Then students enter into a professional class, which, at this point, is easy for them to choose according to their abilities. – A special architecture class is open to strong students, after an exam and submission of pieces demonstrating sufficient capabilities in the area of construction. A preparatory class gradually develops the sensibilities of the students, who then follow the course directed by Prof. Wilhelm Kreis.

These students are generally between the ages of 23 and 26. They receive a superior education, which enables them to undertake monumental building projects. Students from four different German schools of horticulture (Gartenschule) also come to improve themselves in this class. They will become "architects of gardens", a new field that reintroduces principles of architectural organisation, abandoned long ago, into every aspect of gardens. Under Prof. Kreis they study the grand conception of parks or of gardens; they also learn to design small houses such as those of gardeners, guards – outbuildings, pavilions, etc. – Mr Kreis gives his students specified projects, generally developed from the subjects of past competitions – such as: the Leipzig train station, the park in Hamburg, the Wertheim shops, etc., etc. This class gave me a very favourable impression. It is finished with the excesses of the "Jugendstil". Proportion and rhythm are sought above all, and I even observed a return, almost too pronounced, to Louis XIV, to Baroque, to the Empire. This is moreover a general fact in Germany – great wisdom or perhaps premature weakness!

The class of Professor Ehmcke is certainly one of the best that I have seen, specialising in composition, in the development of the book, handwriting, printing and weaving of materials, in posters, in batiks. A loom is installed, and slightly outdated but adequate machines are at the disposal of the bookbinders, the printers and the etchers. A bookbinder comes two mornings per week to teach the techniques of his art. As at the school of Debschitz and at that of Stuttgart, the installation is basic but **sufficient.**

Superb photographs are hung on the walls of the corridors; when they do not reproduce architectural works of the past, they are masterpieces of modern Parisian painting: Degas, Renoir, Manet, Daumier, etc.

The "Kunstgewerbeschule" of Düsseldorf, has become one of the best in Germany, thanks to the tremendous vigour (I am told) that Prof. Peter Behrens brought to it during his years as its director.

ZEICHEN-AKADEMIE zu HANAU

I visited the school of Hanau, expecting to find a very special system of education, since it is the principal school for jewellery and luxury goods in Germany. I rea-lised that the teaching there was banal and academic. I was not acquainted with the famous professor who was there. – I was indeed disappointed: the same professors who had done half of their teaching in styles and revivals ceaselessly repeated: instead of "making the old" we "now make everything modern". And the results said a lot about this sudden about-face. In brief, I saw nothing there worth noting.

STAATLICHE KUNSTGEWERBESCHULE zu HAMBURG

The school of Hamburg, on the contrary, had the opposite effect on me. Its director, Professor Meyer, through his good humour, has the ability to instil tremendous energy throughout the whole school. He has several fundamental principles: for example, to consider the student as a man from the moment of his entry into the school; he consequently gives him complete freedom; he can choose his tasks for himself and execute any project for any purpose.

He takes them on for an initial six months of free consultation. He is anxious above all to confer a very broad general education on them. Since, he says, most of them come from primary school. He can make their way very smooth as they set out on the path of art. He wants to make sure, therefore, that they are never "left behind", and it is for this reason that professors of the first rank (two poets, various professors, etc.) offer the only required course, from eight to nine each morning, on literature, history, physics, etc.

The students attend the school for three or four years, that is to say until they are worthy of a certificate of competence signed by the Director. To excite them about the work, he gives them complete freedom in the choice of their assignments, and the School furnishes models for free. In the same studio I thus saw three models for six students. In a word, the studios are at their disposal from eight in the morning until nine at night. If the student obtains a commission, the school pays for supplies (colours, etc.), but the student is paid for his labour. This concerns, of course, commissions of a special kind – paintings for a library for example, requiring at least a year of work; the student thus receives some 2000 francs from the client.

During my visit, the date of a country fair was approaching. A whole class was actively engaged in the artistic side of the festivities: decorations for triumphal arches, grandstands, costumes, puppet theatres, etc. The women, likewise, were attending to the preparation of marionettes for individual clients.

The technique of drawing live models is new here. It takes place in a class for paintings in buildings, under the direction of Prof. W. von Beckerath, which includes the study of the figure for monumental painting: it seems as if one draws natural grandeur on a sheet stretched upon a frame. The model assumes a convenient pose, sometimes right beside the designers, who have placed their easels wherever it suits them; they have chosen a certain aspect of the model; they are going to dedicate every moment to this one aspect, and, returning to their places, they draw the model as if by heart. The director, Dr Meyer, pretends that the results are amazing. It is evident that the powers of observation are sharpened extraordinarily in this way.

Another method of developing the force of observation is that of cut papers, which both the older and the beginning students practise. The children obtain fantastic, disconcerting results with this technique. It consists in working intuitively and without doing any drawing at all. Sheets of coloured paper and scissors are the only supplies and the only tools. At first they cut trees, people, houses, etc. from a single sheet, then assemble this mosaic, arranging and pasting. They make little pictures out of this, which were all sold in the last exhibition. The children made veritable Gauguins, through the integral and organic line of each thing, through the splendid touch of colour, through naive charm. In this way, they learn the powerful harmonies of colours, audacious reds, blacks, whites and yellows; then they arrive at the highest sense of order, since they observe and juxtapose their motifs in the frame, until achieving balance. Without effort, and simply in the name of curiosity, without compromising a completed composition, they can dare to add a fantastic and unanticipated note. This repeats, but greatly expands, Delacroix's lesson with bars of sealing wax. With colour they learn to see the value of a quick and sharp note or a dominant, powerfully simple one; the sense of vision becomes acute; because cutting out a form without preliminary drawing requires having seen it in order to express it only with contour; little by little, only the synthetic line matters, and besides the charming results attained, the student has gained something else: the keen sense of observation, powerful colour, order.

– The new building for the school is currently being constructed: the budget for it is two million. It will include two innovative greenhouses of 37 m. long and a glazed central hall for the study of plants. A library and a salon for models of all sorts will be open to **the public** (to anyone interested); one will be able to obtain easels there for drawing, stands and clay for modelling.

The ground floor of one of the pavilions will be composed of very large studios; each of these studios will be given to 1, 2, 3 or 4 students who will decorate them; then photographs will be taken of them and the walls washed, in order to be re-used over and over again for the same purpose. Thus the student decorator, constrained until now to compose on the drawing board, will no longer create work that is so often sterile; he will work upon the wall itself, and each stroke of the brush will be a lesson for him.
The school of Hamburg has attracted recognised masters: Prof. Richard Meyer, architect; Prof. Willy Beckerath, painter; Prof. O. Czeschka, painter (invited from the Wiener Werkstätte); Richard Luksch, sculptor; Richard Schmidt, architect.

The school of Hamburg includes a section for the book arts (printing and binding), where remarkable bindings, endpapers and many objects of leatherwork are made. – This section, which promotes modern techniques, receives tradesmen from the city as non-traditional students, and they can complete a serious apprenticeship in six months.

The year-end exhibition is really a sale for the benefit of the students.

UNTERRICHSANSTALT
DES KÖNIGL. KUNSTGEWERBE-MUSEUM BERLIN
(Teaching establishment of the Royal Museum of Decorative Arts)

Direction Prof. Bruno Paul. – Architecture, monumental and decorative sculpture classes, graphic arts and painting classes (Profs. Bruno Paul, Grenander, Wakerle, Orlik, E. R. Weiss)

There is never any question that these are academic projects, but the "method" is less apparent than in Hamburg (I speak here of the very great Viennese influence of Prof. O. Czeschka). Otherwise the same freedom presides over all: no fixed hours; the students make what they want, following the paths of their choice. Moreover, a professor receiving personal commissions (sculpture, painting) can have them executed by his students, whom he pays by the hour or by the job. Likewise, students can undertake their own commissions: "It is important for them to earn something from time to time!" a professor said to me. So, the whole class of applied sculpture is busy with the facade of a "Kunstauktions-Geschäft" (bronze gates, medallions, brackets, standing figures), – others are working on the figures for a bridge (monumental rams). The live ram constitutes part of the school's teaching equipment, along with other fellow creatures such as rabbits, ducks, chickens, fish, etc.

Professors Bruno Paul and Grenander engage their best students practically like employees. With the result that one can enjoy an education, practise in one of the best architecture offices in Germany, and be paid! These students remain there for five or six years; then, one day, they are called to be professors in the provinces.

The building is vast, but the halls are not at all luxurious. Marvellous engravings by Piranesi are hung in the administrators' corridor; in the grand foyer stands a selection of castings from the most beautiful figures of medieval, Greek, Assyrian and Egyptian sculpture. – A cafeteria is available to the students, as well as a garden.

KÖNIGL. SÄCHSISCHE KUNTSGEWERBESCHULE – DRESDEN

Huge building, recently built for a few students (300). And I am told that it will soon be inadequate! A visit to this school taught me nothing. I found the commonplace and the routine there, and because it is not my intention to criticise, but only to say good things, I must satisfy myself with this observation: this is a school, in every sense of the word.

GROSSHERZOGLICHE-SÄCHSISCHE KUNSTGEWERBESCHULE – WEIMAR
Direction Prof. Henry van de Velde

The fundamental principle of the school is this: raise the level of local industries and combat the routine.

It is, therefore, a professional school above all. The most developed disciplines are silver and gold smithing, ceramics, weaving and bookbinding.

Another principle of the school is to avoid teaching students mechanical processes. In spite of appearing irrational, they want to bring back the total craftsmen. Later, these craftsmen will understand how to use machines well and to derive a profit from them.

The works of the students, therefore, are flawlessly executed. They are available for purchase.

Instruction is given solely by the director, Mr H. van de Velde. There is a master craftsman in each class. The education is the most general possible. There is **ornament** first (but never painting, nor drawing of flowers or living models), then composition in every possible area of expertise. Step by step, on his own, the student specialises and chooses his vocation.

The master of apprenticeship, at the end of three or four years, awards the student a diploma of master ceramist, of master carver, master bookbinder, etc. – the exceptional students will then be admitted to the interior architecture class, with a special master, but under the direction of Mr van de Velde.

In one room, however, copying from nature is tolerated. This is limited, it is true, to the interpretive copying of withered and fresh plants in various vases, of lichens and of algae standing out against backgrounds of coloured cloth. The student does not have to copy the design of what he sees, but only the colour, in order to obtain documentation of colour harmonies. This is done in large-scale watercolours, and the results are excellent.

The school furnishes advice and designs without charge to merchants; if an individual requests projects more than once, he must pay for them.

The influence of the school does not appear to me to go beyond the boundaries of the province, which is a reflection of how the programme is designed.

Almost all of the schools have adopted the practice of publishing luxuriously produced brochures and annual reports. The cover is sometimes designed by a student, and numerous illustrations reproduce the work executed during the year. Thus, by comparing these various brochures to a study of the programmes, the courses and their professors, it is easy to ascertain the worth of a school, its tendencies and its practical influence.

Almost all of these schools have begun modestly; the premises that house them attest to this. However, most of them will be radically transformed, because the authorities have felt the profound influence that the new teaching in the applied arts has had on industry and commerce, as well as on the cultural advancement of the nation; and they have understood the advantage to be gained in supporting the efforts of progressive masters.

I have already noted "The School for the Decoration of Shopfronts". One interesting innovation is the foundation of **a Seminar für Städtbau** (school for art in the construction of cities) in the "Technische Hochschule" of Berlin. Its curriculum intends to produce architects for planning departments who will know how to pursue the reforms discussed above in the plans for the expansion of cities.

The lesson that stood out for me in visiting these schools can be summarised in this way: success comes to those who know how to align theoretical teaching with practice, or better still to those who make practice the reason for theoretical considerations. The inverse tendency, this is the regression to **"The School"**, the school that develops feeble attitudes, that develops men living apart from practical life, apart from their age and its needs. It is a school that returns to the cliché, to the masquerade of styles, to the routine.

The tuition fees in the various schools are as follows:

KUNSTGEWERBE-SCHULE – Hamburg: 24 marks per semester for daytime classes (34 marks for the painting section because the pigments are provided by the school), 10 marks for evening and Sunday classes.

UNTERRICHTSANSTALT des KUNSTGEWERBE-MUSEUM – Berlin: 60 marks annually.

LEHR- und VERSUCHS-ATELIERS von Wilhelm Debschitz – Munich: for the course on general culture, 110 marks for the first quarter; 40 marks per month for the next quarter; 35 marks monthly for the rest of the year; 30 marks monthly for 2nd year: 28 marks per month for the 3rd and 4th years.

For the same course and the use of training workshops: 140 marks for the 1st quarter, 50 marks per month for the second quarter, then 45 marks monthly; 40 marks per month for 2nd year; 38 marks per month for 3rd and 4th years.

KUNSTGEWERBESCHULE – Düsseldorf: for daytime classes: summer semester 30 marks; winter 40 marks. For evening courses: summer semester: 10 marks; winter 15 marks. For the architecture class, 150 marks per year. – Foreigners pay quintuple.

GROSSHERZOGLICHE-SÄCHSISCHE KUNSTGEWERBESCHULE – Weimar: 100 marks per year, double for foreigners.

KÖNIGLICHE KUNSTGEWERBESCHULE – Dresden: 60 marks annually; 150 marks for foreigners.

ZEICHEN-AKADEMIE – Hanau: Daytime classes, annually 50 marks; for female students 75 marks. Foreigners pay quintuple.

LEHR- und VERSUCHS-WERKSTÄTTE – Stuttgart: 10 marks entry fee; 30 marks per semester, 50 marks for foreigners.

IV

FINAL CONSIDERATIONS

FINAL CONSIDERATIONS

G ERMANY is organised; chapter II "German Initiatives and Productions" describes the nation's collective economic movement. The consequence of this will be (it is already) a privileged position for German industry among those of other nations. This has also been its rehabilitation: the phrase "it's German" no longer retains its contemptuous significance.

But to argue for art and for everything else, it would seem that this great renewal of applied art in Germany has been above all the overflow of the energies of its people and of its gift for organisation. The role of Art in this has diminished, Art was a pretext, a means, a springboard. It was not, it seems to me, the motive. Also the creative forces exulted momentarily by the violent thrust of external contingencies seem now to be weakening. The artistic spirit having acquired the right of authority suddenly feels its insignificance in the midst of the immense terrain that these last few years have given it to exploit. Troubled, it looks around itself; it has lost its contemplative faith in the past; the secessionist fire has died down, and Germany, for the past one or two years especially, returns to follow the footsteps of the artistic giants of France. The champions of this struggle seem hesitant to capitulate prematurely.

Does one not witness an opposite phenomenon in France? It is undeniable that an enormous amount of energy is consumed in stultifying efforts. Perhaps laborious growth is worthwhile to a plant with deeper roots. Will a France suffocated by Germany escape from its lethargy in the area of applied art? Precursory signs have appeared at the last two "Salons d'Automne". Will the very first innovators, those from forty years ago, finally receive their due?

One may find that I emphasise national rivalries too much here; they are, in fact, ethnic. But they do exist between the two countries; as a Frenchman in Germany I have suffered from them; I have been struck by them in Paris, where they are becoming increasingly evident while also intensifying the German invasion. Incidentally, for each nation these are precious stimulants.

A study such as the one the Commission of the École d'Art has facilitated for me must be undertaken again by others; the remarkable Germany of industrial Art demands to be known. In the hour of international competition, information also must cross borders. Germany is a book about reality. If Paris is the foyer of Art, Germany resides in the great yard of production. Experiments have been undertaken there; the struggles there have been effective: the building is raised and the halls with their historiated walls recount the triumph of order and tenacity.

La Chaux-de-Fonds, January 1912

CH.-É. JEANNERET.

TABLE OF CONTENTS

EDITOR'S NOTE

Alex T. Anderson's translation of the *Étude sur le mouvement d'art décoratif en Allemagne* from the original French publication adheres closely to the author's style and the time around 1910. Jeannert's characteristic features, i.e. typical abbreviations, capitalisation and sentence structure have been retained where possible; only errors, such as mistakes in the spelling of German names, have been corrected. The typesetting also follows the line breaks and elements from the original layout.

Charles-Édouard Jeanneret, Villa Schwob, La Chaux-de-Fonds, 1916/17

SELECTED BIBLIOGRAPHY

Banham, Reyner, *Theory and Design in the First Machine Age*, 2nd edn, MIT Press, Cambridge, Mass., 1960

Brooks, H. Allen, *Le Corbusier's Formative Years*, University of Chicago Press, Chicago and London, 1997

Buddensieg, Tilmann and Henning Rogge, *Industriekultur: Peter Behrens and the AEG, 1907–1914*, trans. Iain Boyd Whyte, The MIT Press, Cambridge, Mass., 1984

Cingria-Vaneyre, Alexandre, *Les entretiens de la villa du rouet: Essais dialogues sur l'art plastique en Suisse romande*, Geneva, 1908

Collegi d'Arquitectes de Catalunya, ed., *Le Corbusier et le Livre*, Actar, Barcelona, 2005

de Smet, Catherine, *Le Corbusier – Architect of Books*, Lars Müller Publishers, Baden, 2005

Dohrn, Wolf, *Die Gartenstadt Hellerau und weitere Schriften*, Hellerau-Verlag, Dresden, 1992 (reprint)

Gresleri, Giuliano, ed., *Le Corbusier, Voyage d'Orient – Carnets*, Electa, Milan/Fondation Le Corbusier, Paris, 1987 (German, Italian and English editions)

Gresleri, Giuliano, *Le Corbusier – Reise nach dem Orient*, Spur Verlag, Zurich, 1991

Gresleri, Giuliano, ed., *Le Corbusier, Les voyages d'Allemagne – Carnets*, Electa, Milan/Fondation Le Corbusier, Paris, 1994 (German, Italian and English editions)

Hegemann, Werner, *Der Städtebau nach den Ergebnissen der allgemeinen Städtebau-Ausstellung in Berlin, mit einem Anhang: Die internationale Städtebau-Ausstellung in Düsseldorf*, Wasmuth, Berlin, 1911

Hesse-Frielinghaus, Herta, ed., et al., *Karl-Ernst Osthaus: Leben und Werk*, Bongers, Recklinghausen, 1971

Ikeda, Yuko, ed., *Vom Sofakissen zum Städtebau – Hermann Muthesius und der Deutsche Werkbund*, Tokyo, 2002

Jeanneret, Charles-Édouard, "L'Art et l'Utilité Publique", in *L'Abeille*, supplement to *National Suisse*, 15 May 1910

Jeanneret, Charles-Édouard, *Étude sur le mouvement d'art décoratif en Allemagne*, La Chaux-de-Fonds, 1912; Da Capo Press, New York, 1968 (reprint)

Jeanneret, Charles-Édouard, "Le renouveau dans l'architecture" in *L'Œuvre*, vol. 1, no. 2, 1914

Jencks, Charles, *Le Corbusier and the Continual Revolution in Architecture*, Monacelli Press, New York, 2000

Jenger, Jean, ed., *Le Corbusier – Choix de lettres*, Birkhäuser, Basel / Boston / Berlin, 2002

Junghanns, Kurt, *Der Deutsche Werkbund – Sein erstes Jahrzehnt*, Henschelverlag, Berlin, 1982

Kleihues, Josef Paul, et al., *Bauen in Berlin 1900–2000*, Nicolai, Berlin, 2000

Le Corbusier, *L'Art décoratif d'aujourd'hui*, Crès, Paris 1925; trans. James I. Dunnett as *The Decorative Art of Today*, Architectural Press, London, 1987

Le Corbusier, *Voyage d'Orient*, Forces Vives, Paris, 1966

Moos, Stanislaus von, *Le Corbusier: Elements of a Synthesis*, The MIT Press, Cambridge, Mass., 1979

Moos, Stanislaus von, and Arthur Rüegg, *Le Corbusier before Le Corbusier*, Yale University Press, New Haven and London, 2002

Nerdinger, Winfried, "Standard und Typ: Le Corbusier und Deutschland 1920–1927", in Stanislaus von Moos, ed., *L'Esprit Nouveau – Le Corbusier und die Industrie*, Ernst und Sohn, Berlin/Zurich, 1987

Oechslin, Werner, "Allemagne: Influences, confluences et reniements", in Jacques Lucan, ed., *Le Corbusier – Une encyclopédie*, Centre Georges Pompidou, Paris, 1987

Schulze-Naumburg, Paul, *Kulturarbeiten*, 9 vols, Callwey, Munich, 1901–17

Schwartz, Frederic J., *The Werkbund. Design Theory and Mass Culture before the First World War*, Yale University Press, New Haven and London 1996

Sitte, Camillo, *Der Städtebau nach seinen künstlerischen Grundsätzen*, Graeser, Vienna, 1889

Stamm, Rainer, *Karl Ernst Osthaus – Reden und Schriften*, Verlag der Buchhandlung Walther König, Cologne, 2002

Stürmer, Michael, *Das ruhelose Reich*, Siedler, Munich, 1983

Thiersch, August, *Die Proportionen in der Architektur*, Diehl, Munich, 1883

DATE DUE